"What a daring and needed book! Actually, this is more than a book; it's a weapon that will help you kill the enemy of mediocrity by challenging you to use the discipline of spiritual discernment through life's gray areas. Brent Crowe provides the arsenal to wage war against a lukewarm faith. Thank you, Brent, for daring to tackle these controversial issues in such a bold and biblically centered way."

— DAVID NASSER, pastor, Christ City Church,
Birmingham, Alabama; author and speaker

"The tension between liberty and license has long been something the body of Christ has wrestled with. How do we avoid legalism without losing the strength of our convictions? In *Chasing Elephants*, Brent Crowe does a fantastic job of unraveling this question so that anyone can make applications to his or her everyday life. He gives key principles for decision making in relation to some very complex issues today's Christ follower faces and is especially helpful in providing guidance as to what a Christian is to do when the Bible doesn't address an issue specifically. I highly recommend this book. It is a much-needed resource in today's confusing moral climate."

— DAVID LANDRITH, senior pastor, Long Hollow Baptist Church,
Hendersonville, Tennessee

1-18-15

CHASING ELEPHANTS

WRESTLING WITH THE GRAY AREAS OF LIFE

BRENT CROWE

Discipleship Inside Out™

NAVPRESS
Discipleship Inside Out™

NavPress is the publishing ministry of The Navigators, an international Christian organization and leader in personal spiritual development. NavPress is committed to helping people grow spiritually and enjoy lives of meaning and hope through personal and group resources that are biblically rooted, culturally relevant, and highly practical.

For a free catalog go to www.NavPress.com
or call 1.800.366.7788 in the United States or 1.800.839.4769 in Canada.

ISBN-13: 978-1-61521-121-0

Cover design by Faceout Studio, Jeff Miller

Some of the anecdotal illustrations in this book are true to life and are included with the permission of the persons involved. All other illustrations are composites of real situations, and any resemblance to people living or dead is coincidental.

Unless otherwise identified, all Scripture quotations in this publication are taken from The Holy Bible, English Standard Version (ESV), copyright © 2001 by Crossway Bibles, a division of Good News Publishers. Used by permission. All rights reserved. Other versions used include: the New King James Version (NKJV). Copyright © 1982 by Thomas Nelson, Inc. Used by permission. All rights reserved; *THE MESSAGE* (MSG). Copyright © 1993, 1994, 1995, 1996, 2000, 2001, 2002. Used by permission of NavPress Publishing Group; the New American Standard Bible® (NASB), Copyright © 1960, 1962, 1963, 1968, 1971, 1972, 1973, 1975, 1977, 1995 by The Lockman Foundation. Used by permission; the *Holy Bible, New International Version®* (NIV®), Copyright © 1973, 1978, 1984 by International Bible Society, used by permission of Zondervan, all rights reserved; and the *Contemporary English Version* (CEV) copyright © 1995 by American Bible Society. Used by permission.

Library of Congress Cataloging-in-Publication Data

Crowe, Brent, 1978-
  Chasing elephants : wrestling with the gray areas of life / Brent Crowe.
    p. cm.
  ISBN 978-1-61521-121-0
  1. Christian ethics. 2. Christian life. I. Title.
  BJ1251.C82 2010
  241--dc22
                          2010010406

Printed in the United States of America

3 4 5 6 7 8 / 14 13 12 11

To Christina . . . thanks for the dance.

CONTENTS

ACKNOWLEDGMENTS

My first thank you is to Christina, without whom I could not imagine my life or ministry. God's goodness and grace are daily evidenced in your love for me. And to my children: Gabriel, Charis, and Mercy . . . you are the true calling of my life.

I am grateful to my godly parents, Roy and Karen Crowe, who instilled in me a passion for studying the Scriptures. To Jay and Diane Strack—Jay, thanks for letting me be your tag-team partner with Student Leadership University. To Nannie, my favorite author.

To the team at SLU, it is a privilege to minister with you in helping this generation *Think, Dream, and Lead*. To Kenika, your leadership in the details is amazing. And to the thousands of students we serve, watching you *seek first the kingdom* is overwhelming and motivating.

To my mentors in ministry: Dad, "Rick Flair," David Nasser, Scott Dawson, Bob Reccord, Kelly Green, Andrew Oates, and Chuck Allen. Thank you for your godly example and investment in my life. To Michael Catt, thanks for getting me in a headlock and saying, "This must be a book." To Bill Brown, you taught me the importance of having a biblical worldview. To Danny Aken and Alvin Reid, I am indebted to what you have taught me. To Tommy Graham, who made it possible for me to go to college. To Matt, a younger brother with wisdom beyond my years.

THE JOURNEY IS FREEDOM

I have a dog, although I don't really know why. He eats constantly and is scared of everything, and I mean everything! He would knock over elderly people and children to get out of the way of an oncoming shadow. He needs a dog whisperer, an animal psychic, or Dr. Phil because I'm out of ideas on how to change his behavior. One of the more intelligent activities that consumes his time is the nightly chasing of the tail. This ritual is so meaningless that I can't help but watch.

Does life ever feel that way? Circular, boring, and meaningless at times? I choose to believe that God never meant for life to be a meaningless routine of living out our days going in circles, bored to death with the predictable nature of it all.

For most of my life, I was taught what to believe. I was even told why I believed what I believed. Recently though, I awakened to an unfortunate reality: *I have never taken the time to learn "how to believe."* I was always told to "land the plane" on various issues of life. The problem was that no one, including myself, had ever built a landing strip, which meant that I continually crashed and burned. Of course, I'm not talking about the main principles of the Christian faith but about hundreds of gray areas. Those matters of life that the Bible doesn't specifically address and preachers don't like to preach about. Issues like entertainment choices, operating in the cyber world, humanitarian efforts, social drinking, language, tattoos, and the list goes on.

While some of these gray issues might seem trivial, they often become the elephant in the room—that big and attention-catching behemoth that no one wants to tackle or deal with, so everyone pretends not to see it. That way, no one has to be challenged to make decisions about it.

What would God have us believe about all of the moral and ethical elephants we come face-to-trunk with? Are we left to fend for ourselves and therefore should accept a certain amount of ambiguity?

Following Jesus is a daring adventure that each of us must choose personally. No part of the adventure is more important than this central reality of the Christian faith: the cross. And there seems to be no word that captures the intoxicating emotion the Christian feels better than . . . *freedom*.

Christ has set us free to live a free life! Jesus both sets us free and enables us to live free. A proper understanding of this freedom can help us know what to believe in the gray areas of life and be fully convinced in our own minds. This conviction then brings us to a place where, instead of ignoring the elephants in the room, we can readily address them.

As we'll discover, freedom is both a journey and a responsibility, and it provides motivation and direction, clarity and mystery. Ultimately, freedom involves finding that you must be exhaustively intentional about capturing the moments of life as well as willing to wrestle with anything that seems confusing. However, we can be certain that no gray issue, or elephant, is so large (or so small) that it can't be devoured one bite at a time when looking through the grid of Scripture.

FREEDOM DEFINED

Before we try to understand how to live a free life in Christ, we first need a working definition of what *freedom* is. Of course, we'll expand on this definition as we move forward, but let's go back to Creation and capture the very essence of this God-given gift of freedom. Following the introduction of man to the world, God placed Adam in the Garden of Eden to tend and keep it. "And the LORD God commanded the man, saying, 'Of every tree of the garden you may freely eat; but of the tree of the knowledge of good and evil you shall not eat, for in the day that you eat of it you shall surely die'" (Genesis 2:16-17, NKJV).

Three distinguishing components are evident in the way God defined Adam's freedom in the garden:

1. A **respect** for the authority of God's words: "And the LORD God commanded the man."
2. A **responsibility** to stay within the boundaries outlined by the words of God: "Of every tree of the garden you may freely eat; but of the tree of the knowledge of good and evil you shall not eat."
3. **Consequences** for crossing the stated boundaries: "In the day that you eat of it you shall surely die."[1]

Shortly after this command comes the temptation and fall of mankind into sin. The temptation occurs when the Devil appears in the form of a serpent and asks Eve, "Has God indeed said, 'You shall not eat of every tree of the garden'?" (Genesis 3:1, NKJV). While God has already painted a picture of what it means to live happy and free, Adam and Eve's response paints a picture of freedom mishandled and eventually lost. Genesis 3:1-13 then provides the unfolding narrative of a downward slide into sin:

- Doubt and denial of the words of God (verses 1-4)
- Replacement of truth with experience (verses 4-5)
- A sense of entitlement (verse 5)
- The desire to have equality with God (verses 5-6)
- Mankind's first experience with shame (verses 7-10)
- A victim's mentality (verses 11-13)

The story of the first man and woman is indeed grim. Yet it's a story that we all share.

Although mankind's fall results in lasting consequences, God also provides redemption through the promise of Jesus (see Genesis 3:15). This little verse once served as a beacon of hope for generation after generation that One was coming who would set the captives free. Thank God the story of *us* doesn't end with *us* or we would live doomed to suffer guilt and condemnation.

I'm personally grateful for God's provision of redemption and its resulting freedom. You see, I was drowning in guilt and condemnation because I'd made knowing God more about morality than transformation. The problem with this worldview is that it reduces Christianity to rules and regulations that eventually lead to boredom and a sense of entitlement. All the while I failed to recognize the choices I was making were actually the chains that were binding me. Only when I came to the end of me did I find myself face-to-face with the relentless grace of God—and that's when I realized Jesus had set me free.

WHAT LIES AHEAD

The pages to follow are designed to help you, as a follower of Jesus, know how to believe with a deep sense of appreciation for freedom, just as I have found.

In chapters 1–4, we'll dig into four of the longest biblical texts discussing freedom: 2 Corinthians 5:17-21; Romans 14:1–15:13; 1 Corinthians 10:23–11:1; and Galatians 5. As we examine the freedom that we have in Christ, we'll take an in-depth look at each of these passages. At times I'll explain certain Greek words or historical contexts. In this part of the book, we won't address any gray issues or elephants in the room. I want God's Word to imprint on your mind and prepare your heart. This can only happen separate from any baggage or bias that we might have about certain issues.

In chapter 5, we'll take all that we've extracted from Scripture about freedom and place it into a series of questions that I call the "how to believe" grid.

In chapters 6–10, we'll apply certain questions to some elephants in the room: homosexuality, the cyber world, social drinking, entertainment, and humanitarian efforts. You might think of these as case studies for using the questions of the "how to believe" grid about any other elephants in your room.

So, now we proceed with a sacred respect for the words of God, an understanding of responsibility, and a realization of consequences if freedom is mishandled.

Therefore, if it is your own experience and not someone else's
you desire . . .

If you seek to be intentional about the life you've been given . . .

If there is room in your life for both clarity and mystery . . .

If you desire to move beyond "what" and "why" to "how to believe" . . .

Then this book was written for you.

CHAPTER 1

REFRIGERATOR ART

Do you remember when you were a child and got dropped off at Sunday school or day care? You probably had story time, snack time, and—of course—arts and crafts!

During this creative time, you had the opportunity to make a work of art using nothing more than crayons, construction paper, glitter, and glue. For most of us, this time intoxicated the mind and soul with endless creative possibilities that could only result in a masterpiece destined to take its place among history's greatest works of art! Or maybe that was just the way I felt after eating the glue.

Most kids choose to draw a picture of their house, pet, or family. Of course, houses aren't really made of pizza, dogs don't have six legs, and grandpa isn't blue. Yet in the mind of the artists, they create masterpieces.

When I was a kid and drew these pictures, I was so excited for my mom or dad to come pick me up. Then I could officially present them with my artistic creation as a token of affection and appreciation. Of course, what I thought to be a masterpiece more realistically represented Picasso on drugs.

The anticipation leading up to the presentation of my picture to my parents climaxed with their celebratory affirmation of how glorious it was. Some time ago, the cynical side of me concluded that this was further proof that all parents lie to their children for their own good. But now that I am a parent of three, I realize that parenting is a role requiring me to celebrate the best my three-and-a-half-year-old can do for someone his age.

In fact, at this very moment, I'm in my home office and my children are at the kitchen table drawing pictures of things that only make sense to them. I just overheard my son yell with joyful anticipation to my wife, "I want to show Daddy!" And when I receive his picture, I will do with it what my parents and millions of others have done: *put it on the refrigerator.* Until I became a dad, I could never understand why parents display their kids' art in such an odd place. But now I know that the refrigerator is the most visited and prominent place in the house.

Why am I talking about refrigerator art? Because in the end, the best I can offer God is nothing more than refrigerator art! As odd as it may sound, this needs to be the starting point for our discussion on freedom in Christ. In fact, before we can even begin to evaluate freedom, we must first understand what it means to be "in Christ."

To be "in Christ" infers that someone was moved to such a position at a specific time by a specific cause. It might help to imagine a circle that represents your life. Before Christ, the circle is empty. But when you become a Christian, the circle is filled with all that Christ is.[1] It might sound topsy-turvy, but to be in Christ also means that Christ is in you.

When your life was empty, the best you could offer God was but filthy rags (see Isaiah 64:6) because you were spiritually dead in your sins (see Ephesians 2:1). But then, at a specific time, the grace of God caused your position to change. This has been correctly referred to as your salvation experience. When you realized you were empty and that you wanted Christ to step out of heaven and into your life to make you free, what could you have possibly offered to God? Do you think your talents, money, cultural status, or anything else impressed him? You see, I don't think the Father has ever looked at the Son and said, "Boy, are we lucky to have that person."

The truth is that we have nothing to offer God but empty and messed-up lives without purpose. In other words, refrigerator art.

One of the most astonishing aspects of God's grace is that he doesn't bring us close to him just so we can be like dogs waiting to feast off the scraps that might fall from his table. No, our new position is "in Christ," providing us with the most valued position and purpose. While "the best we can offer God is refrigerator art" might sound like a pessimistic idea at first, I hope that on further reflection you see that it screams the overwhelming grace of a God who welcomes us into relationship with himself.

One portion of Scripture that speaks to this concept is 2 Corinthians 5:17-21:

> Therefore, if anyone is in Christ, he is a new creation. The old has passed away; behold, the new has come. All this is from God, who through Christ reconciled us to Himself and gave us the ministry of reconciliation; that is, in Christ God was reconciling the world to Himself, not counting their trespasses against them, and entrusting to us the message of reconciliation. Therefore, we are ambassadors for Christ, God making His appeal through us. We implore you on behalf of Christ, be reconciled to God. For our sake He made Him to be sin who knew no sin, so that in Him we might become the righteousness of God.

If our entire identity can be summarized with the phrase "in Christ," then we must understand the following realities. Understanding these realities and confessing them with our lives will inevitably serve as a gateway to understanding freedom.

THE REALITY OF A LIFE MADE FREE: WE ARE NEW CREATIONS

The first reality of a life made free involves the life we experience as a new creation in Christ. This naturally leads us to ask, "What does it mean to be a new creation?"

The word *new* is translated from the Greek word *kainos*, which is "metaphorically speaking of Christians who are renewed and changed from evil to good by the Spirit of God (2 Corinthians 5:17; Galatians 6:15; Ephesians 4:24); a new heart, a transformed, saved heart."[2] The word for *creation* is translated from the Greek word *ktisis*, which means "no mere mending or improvement but an actual 'creation.' The word means the act of creating and is then applied also to what the act creates."[3]

At first glance, these terms might remind us of the creation language used in Genesis. The comparison holds true in that God created something completely new; he didn't simply upgrade or improve on an already existing life. Theologian John Wesley said, "Only the power that makes a world can make a Christian."[4] This is essential in our understanding of God, because the sacrificial love of Christ is not to reform morals but to transform, not to improve life but to grant life to all.

However, the comparison between the creation of the world and the creation of a Christian does fall short. The creation that took place "in the beginning" was characterized by God's all-powerfulness. But the new creation of an individual spiritually is characterized by God's grace. Understanding what it means to be a new creation is vitally important to understanding freedom in Christ; if you don't understand your identity, then you'll inevitably have a distorted view of freedom.

Because we are new creations, "the old has passed away." We can best understand what this means in light of Romans 6:11, where the apostle Paul wrote, "You also must consider yourselves dead to sin and alive to God in Christ Jesus." This verse speaks to the end of an era in a new believer's life. The era of serving sinful self is over, and we're born into a new era where our goal is Christ. The phrase "has passed away" refers to a defining moment in time or a decisive act when life is liberated and made into a new creation.

Being a new creation also means "behold, the new has come." Paul used the term *behold*, which serves to call attention to something.[5] He was placing an exclamation point on something he hadn't stated yet. This helps his audience realize the huge consequences of what he is sharing. John Wesley commented on the phrase "the new has come":

> He has a new life, new senses, new faculties, new affections, new appetites, new ideas and conceptions. His whole tenor of action and conversation is new, and he lives, as it were, in a new world. God, men, the whole creation, heaven, earth, and all therein, appear in a new light, and stand related

to him in a new manner, since he was created anew in Christ Jesus.[6]

When I have the chance to lead someone in a prayer asking Jesus to save him or her, I like to ask a very simple question: "How do you feel?" I ask the question this way because it seems to weed out any churchy or religious jargon and allows the person to express his or her feelings in an honest fashion.

A few years ago, I was preaching at a camp on the West Coast. After the evening service, a girl in the eighth grade came running up to me yelling, "Camp pastor, camp pastor, stop! I need to talk to you!"

I turned around and asked how I could help.

Her response was, "I just wanted to tell you tonight I asked Jesus into my heart and life."

While this was amazing news and I truly rejoiced with her decision, I recognized that she was using the same language I was using. So I asked her how she felt about her decision.

For a few moments, she stood in front of me speechless, searching for the right words to describe the amazing experience of salvation. Then her eyes looked at me as if they had discovered the perfect answer to such a question and she asked, "Have you ever seen the Pepsi commercial?"

Caught off guard, I looked back and said, "I've seen a few."

She responded, "Have you ever seen the one where there is an old Pepsi can machine, and it unzips from the top to the bottom and a new Pepsi can machine comes out? That's what has happened to me!"

To this day, I believe that is the most theologically correct description of salvation I've ever heard.

On another occasion, I spent the better part of a night with two drug dealers, sharing Jesus with them in their home. Throughout the night, as we sat in their den discussing what it means to have a relationship with God, I kept noticing this large black marble table in the middle of the den. It didn't look like a normal coffee table because of how big it was and how low to the ground it sat. Finally, after hours of discussion, we knelt at that table, and they prayed to begin a relationship with Jesus. After a time of prayer, we sat back, and I asked one of them how he felt. He looked at that black table and explained to me that every night it would be white with cocaine and other drugs and they kneel at the table and get high. He looked at me with tears in his eyes and said, "You want to know how I feel? Tonight I kneeled at this table, and now I feel new."

The astonishing and relentless grace of God can reach a rich girl from the valley who seems to have everything or an addict who would sell everything just to get his next high. God's desire for both of them is the same: to make them new creations in Christ.

"New creation" is a position that never grows old. It's not like one day we could ever be "old creations in Christ Jesus." Why? Because every morning God's "lovingkindness is better than life" (Psalm 63:3, NASB). And the result is that my life can't help but be about worship.

Lam 3:22-23 God's lovingkindness or mercies are new every morning

THE REASON FOR A LIFE MADE FREE: *we are a new*
THE LOVE OF GOD *The new with the new Creation*
every morning - new
with God.

The second aspect of a life made free has to do with the love of God, which is woven throughout all of 2 Corinthians 5:17-21. Every verse speaks in some manner directly to God's sacrificial love for humanity. Paul stated that "all this is from God," meaning everything he had stated in the preceding verses. Then Paul elaborated by writing that God "in Christ God was reconciling the world to himself, not counting their trespasses against them, and entrusting to us the message of reconciliation."

We need to analyze two terms here to further understand the love of God. The first word, which is the central idea, is *reconciliation*. Paul is the only author in the New Testament to use the noun *reconciliation* and the verb *to reconcile*.[7] The picture Paul painted is God reconciling man to himself, and wrapped up in that is the ministry of reconciliation. This is significant because Paul demonstrated a natural relationship between being (in Christ) and doing (the ministry of reconciliation). In other words, if I *am* something, then I *will do* something. The motive for Christian living is that Jesus on the cross rescued sinners; while he is without sin, he never turns away sinners who come to him. Being messengers of reconciliation is actually part of our identity in Christ as believers. Motive and ministry are born together at the conversion experience.

Theologian Wayne Grudem defined *reconciliation* as "the removal of enmity and the restoration of fellowship between two parties."[8] More specifically, *reconciliation* is "the divine work of redemption denoting that act of redemption insofar as God Himself is concerned by taking upon Himself our sin and becoming an atonement. Thus a relationship of peace with mankind is established which was hitherto prevented by the demands of His justice."[9] In other words, we are no longer condemned and enslaved individuals, but we have been rescued and set free in Jesus Christ. Paul wrote more about this in 1 Corinthians 15:3-4: "Christ died for our sins, as the Scriptures say. He was buried, and three days later he was raised to life, as the Scriptures say" (CEV).

Reconciliation can only take place when we realize our sins are what put Jesus to death. This is again emphasized in 2 Corinthians 5:21: "For our sake he made Him to be sin who knew no sin." In both 1 Corinthians 15:3 and 2 Corinthians 5:21, the term *for* could be translated "because of." This emphasizes that Christ died both for and because of our sins. I find it a helpful exercise to place my name in verse 21: For *Brent's* sake He made Him to be sin who knew no sin, so that in him *Brent* might become the righteousness of God." Try that with your name and see if it changes the way you understand this concept.

The second term that helps us better understand God's love at work toward us is "not counting." Some translations use the term "not imput-ing." Simply put, God hasn't kept an account of our transgressions. Even though the depravity of mankind created what seems to be an unbridge-able gulf between God and man, *imputation* [handwritten: not imputing] means that "God wiped clean the register of transgressions through Christ's death. The files containing the records of our shortcomings and offenses have been deleted."[10]

Because of imputation — [handwritten: not imputing] or rather because of the debt and enmity that had been built up due to humanity's transgressions and because of the demand of God's holy law—reconciliation is God's solution to humanity's problem.

THE RESPONSIBILITY OF A LIFE MADE FREE: THE MINISTRY OF RECONCILIATION

We just looked at our reconciliation to God through Christ Jesus. However, God also wants to involve us in his agenda: to reconcile others to him. This "ministry of reconciliation" is an integral part of being reconciled to God and being in Christ. While it might seem a bit odd to discuss the idea of helping others cross the line of faith in conjunction with the topic of freedom in Christ, we'll discover in the following chapters that freedom in Christ motivates us to influence those around us with what is good. Christian freedom is not passive, but proactive. It's about recognizing the effects of our choices not only on ourselves but on others. In this context, Paul focused on the proactive or mission-minded side of being in Christ. The eighteenth-century preacher and evangelist George Whitefield called the ministry of reconciliation "the great errand upon which gospel ministers are sent."[11] *Gospel ministers* refers to all of us who are in Christ, and the ministry of reconciliation should find ownership with us from the conception of our spiritual birth.

The apostle Paul stated, "We are ambassadors for Christ, as though God were pleading through us" (2 Corinthians 5:20, NKJV). The contemporary understanding of an ambassador is someone who represents a state or country in a foreign land. The individual has all of the authority of the state he represents backing his presence in the country where he serves.

If you know about Paul and his background, you might recognize a natural pride when he wrote of being an ambassador. Prior to his conversion experience, the apostle was a Jew by culture and religion; he was educated in a prestigious Greek university; and he enjoyed the benefits of being a Roman citizen. His entire life God was preparing him to be a messenger to the world about the gospel of God. So here, he called all those who follow Jesus to be representatives of Christ—individuals operating on the behalf of Christ and carrying the message of reconciliation.

Paul then described the attitude we should have as messengers and representatives for Christ. Being an ambassador involves God making his appeal through us to others who need to be reconciled to Christ. We are called to implore or plead with others to choose reconciliation with God. The term *implore* can also be translated as "beseech, desire, beckon, ask, or beg."[12] From all of these words, we get a profound sense of urgency that must burn within the messenger and originates in the heart of God.

One New Testament scholar wrote that the word *implore* "is remarkable in every way in this connection. Here the God of heaven and of earth and Christ, his Son who by his death reconciled all to God, and here are their high ambassadors representing God in Christ. On the other hand are the transgressors. And lo, these ambassadors are sent by God and Christ to *beg* these transgressors: 'Be reconciled!'"[13]

Here's one way to think about the necessary urgency for delivering the message God has given us. Imagine you are texting a friend and make plans to hang out. As you approach his house to pick him up, you see black smoke rushing out of the downstairs windows. You feel panic because you know that your friend is upstairs playing video games. Would you just casually drive on by and think, *Oh well, guess I better find someone else to hang out with. That guy is toast.* Of course not! You would do whatever was possible to rescue your friend from death. That's the urgency of delivering God's message of reconciliation! The house is on fire, and people all around us are doomed to eternity separated from God if we don't warn them to reconcile with him while they still can.

This quick exploration of 2 Corinthians 5:17-21 is vital to properly understanding the freedom we have in Christ. We need to know clearly what it means to be "in Christ." Many people mistakenly view God as a taskmaster holding Christians on a leash rather than seeing him as the initiator of salvation. We can find the correct perspective about God in 1 John 4:19: "We love because God loved us first" (CEV). This perspective also has a significant impact on our attitude toward our freedom because we understand that God's love is a motivation for our freedom.

Freedom in Christ begins not with what you are allowed to *do,* but with who you are allowed to *be.*

CHAPTER 2

MEAT, IDOLS, AND SPECIAL DAYS

A friend of mine, Julia, grew up in a very structured institutional church. For years, she was taught that people could only pray certain sanctioned prayers and that proper behavior in church was anything but relaxed or joyful.

When Julia was sixteen, a friend invited her to attend a service at her church. Never having attended a different church, Julia was intrigued and curious and agreed to go. What she discovered was a casual atmosphere of Bible study that included humor, strange songs, people who seemed to be happy to be there, and prayers more relational than ritual in nature. Julia was used to religion on cue where each service could be predicted down to the last minute. But this church seemed irreverent in light of her upbringing. As the service concluded and she was leaving, the pastor thanked her for coming. She immediately responded that she wouldn't be back and she would never be a part of a church like this. Then she left.

Years later, as Julia reflected on that experience and shared her story with me, it's obvious that she left her friend's church in the same manner she entered: imprisoned. She allowed the traditions of her home church to prevent her from enjoying the company of other Christians. She was the weak believer Paul described in Romans 14. She left the church building that day empty of the joy and freedom she observed in the others around her because she made mountains out of molehills. Or to borrow the title of one of Shakespeare's plays, Julia made *Much Ado About Nothing*.

People have always made mountains out of molehills and treated trival issues as major ones. For example, some Christians have thought that having a pool table in your house, playing cards, or listening to any non-Christian music was evil. Growing up as the son of a Baptist pastor, I observed certain traditions that were considered sacred cows and nonnegotiable. These traditions included the way people dressed when coming to church or the type of music and instruments considered acceptable during the worship service. In more recent times, Christians have held strongly differing opinions over social drinking and even social networking. We'll look at both of these topics in coming chapters.

As a Christian, your freedom is a powerful, sacred, and even mysterious trust given by God. If we don't seek to properly understand our freedom in Christ, we can cause division and hurt within the Christian community and be poor representatives of Christ to those outside the faith.

So far, we've concluded that the journey to understanding freedom in Christ begins with *being* rather than *doing*. It's about your identity much more than your actions. Now we'll focus on morally debatable issues or what many people call the "gray areas" of life. As I mentioned earlier, I like to think of these issues as the elephants in the room. Sometimes, it seems that no one knows how to deal with these topics. Some people will ignore them, pretending they're not there. Others are more than willing to talk circles around them without making any firm decisions.

I hope you'll make an amazing discovery as you keep reading: *Differences over secondary issues or gray areas should actually unite rather than divide us.* In Romans 14:1–15:13, Paul provided case studies, cautioned us about some boundaries, and demonstrated that properly embracing Christian freedom will produce a life that mirrors the attitude of Christ.

CASE STUDIES IN CHRISTIAN FREEDOM

In Romans 14:1-12, Paul wrote to believers in the church at Rome who were "strong in the faith" versus those who were "weak in the faith." Those who were weak believed they were bound to certain dietary restraints and had to observe a certain day as more holy than others. Those who were strong had a healthy understanding of their freedom so they didn't feel bound by dietary restrictions and they respected all days in the same manner.

Paul began with the command to "receive one who is weak in the faith" (verse 1, NKJV). The idea is to receive or admit into one's society and fellowship, and to treat that individual with kindness.[1] Note that Paul first addressed—as he always did—the strong believer. Paul was emphasizing that strong believers bear a great responsibility to focus on community and not allow division to take place over a difference of opinions.

So why are some people weak in their faith while others are strong? Paul provided two examples concerning pre-Christian customs that help answer this question.

Dietary Restrictions

Paul's first example addresses dietary restrictions that some Roman Christians were struggling with: "One person believes he may eat anything, while the weak person eats only vegetables" (verse 2). The weak Christians didn't fully appreciate what it meant to be part of the New Covenant, as evidenced by the fact that they wouldn't eat meat. They still saw themselves as bound by the Old Testament. The word *testament* means "covenant"; a modern understanding of covenant is the word *agreement*. The Old Testament is the old series of covenants or agreements that God made with his people. The New Testament consists of only one covenant: Jesus.

The weak in their faith found themselves trying to live in the world of two covenants. Many Christians in Rome struggled with this double life, especially relating to dietary laws from pre-Christian days. In fact, in the two centuries prior to Paul, many Jews lost their lives for refusing to eat certain food, such as pork, which the Greeks thought was delicious.[2] Therefore, many who had adhered to customs of the Old Testament law their entire lives weren't willing to leave those customs behind now that they were in Christ.

While we don't necessarily struggle with following dietary laws from the Old Testament today, I believe the motivation for abstaining from meat thousands of years ago still exists in a similar way today. Let me explain.

Those who are weak in the faith have always believed that Christianity is *a thing you do*. They are imprisoned by traditions they believe will make them holy and acceptable to God. I heard Bill Hybels, the pastor of Willow Creek Community Church, say in a sermon on this subject: "The weak Christian is wed to a rule-oriented, mechanical-type faith." Simply put, at some level, people who are weak in their faith are trying to earn a relationship with God. When we base our relationship with God on morality or rules rather than transformation, we will constantly judge ourselves on what we can accomplish rather than what Christ has already accomplished in us.

Paul next issued a firm warning to those both weak and strong in the faith: "Let not the one who eats despise the one who abstains, and let not the one who abstains pass judgment on the one who eats, for God has welcomed him" (verse 3). Theologian and reformer John Calvin explained that Paul "wisely and suitably meets the faults of both parties" by identifying two dangers.[3]

First, Paul addressed the strong believers. A great outward responsibility accompanies those who have discovered what it means to be free from the bondage of legalism. So the first danger and warning was addressed to the strong in the faith not to despise or treat with contempt. The apostle Paul was very explicit that freedom in Christ doesn't breed a sense of arrogance; our freedom doesn't give us the right to look down our spiritual noses at others who haven't yet attained the same freedom. As we'll see in the following verses and other texts, Christian freedom should breed the attitude of Christ and cause us to have compassion on others, not judgment.

The second danger was addressed to the weak, warning them not to judge the strong. In this case, the word *judge* means "to value opinions over relationship." In other words, the weak often make it their goal to be right rather than to build community. Paul was speaking of a critical attitude when a weaker believer wishes to judge or criticize a stronger Christian. The weaker individual doesn't understand the freedom that the stronger person is enjoying; the weaker believer concludes that what's wrong for him must be wrong for everyone.

The statement that Paul used at the end of Romans 14:3 — "for God has welcomed him" — applies to both weak and strong believers. It's sinful for the strong or the weak — or even those who just think they are strong — not to accept and fellowship with one another. If God receives both those who are weak and strong in the faith, what right does any believer have to discriminate against other believers?

In verse 4, Paul reminded us that all of us — whether we are among the weak or strong in the faith — are absolutely desperate for the Lord in order to have any strength to stand at all! <u>The Lord is able and we aren't.</u> This reality should motivate the way we live out our lives as believers and allow us to operate within freedom.

Special Days

Paul's second example, beginning in Romans 14:5, has to do with the custom of some days being more holy than others: "One person esteems one day as better than another, while another esteems all days alike."

Some Christians in Rome considered certain days as more sacred than others because the Old Testament law declared that feast days were set apart to God in a special way. The Sabbath, for example, had particular rules and regulations to follow.[4] A Scottish theologian said it well: "The Jews had made a tyranny of the Sabbath, surrounding it with a jungle of regulations and prohibitions. It was not that Paul wished to wipe out the Lord's Day — far from it; but he did fear an attitude which in effect believed that Christianity consisted in observing one particular day."[5]

Note that Paul didn't take sides about this issue; rather he stated, "Each one should be fully convinced in his own mind" (verse 5). Paul didn't choose sides because both those who adhere to customs of sacred days and those who don't all act "in honor of the Lord" (verse 6). For Paul to take sides regarding this issue would have been inconsistent with the central idea he was communicating: that Christians shouldn't judge each other in such issues, but rather should be fully convinced personally of the positions they hold. <u>The opinions themselves carry no weight and are insignificant.</u> Paul said that what is significant is "if we live, we live to the Lord; and if we die, we die to the Lord. Therefore, whether we live or die, we are the Lord's" (verse 8, NKJV).

In verses 5 through 9, Paul used the word *Lord* seven times. The principle that Paul communicated here is powerful: *Even in issues we find difficult, Christ is still Lord.* This is why I'm convinced that there should never be any neutral or passive areas in a believer's life. When it comes to decisions that are a matter of opinion, it still comes down to whether or not you do something in honor of the Lord. Attitude and purpose can take center stage on whether or not a decision is sin. If you observe one day as more holy than another but do so for selfish reasons and not to honor the Lord, then that's sin. If you respect all days the same for selfish reasons, for example, as out of laziness and not to honor the Lord, then that's sin.

While observing holy days seems irrelevant to us now, we can apply the principles to deal with issues we face today. Again, we'll explore some of these issues, or elephants, in the second half of this book. For example, we'll discover that Jesus is Lord in our social networking and when deciding what movie to watch. This simple fact means that when we focus on judging others or when we act arrogantly, we take away from the focus we should have — that he is Lord and we live unto him.

Much of freedom in Christ is about perspective. Really understanding what it means to be in Christ will compel you to be motivated by grace and not distracted with issues that others are dealing with that you have no business questioning anyway. This doesn't mean that we never focus on other believers; rather, it means we do so with the attitude of honoring Christ in the process.

In the end we must answer for ourselves before God. These two case studies in Romans 14 demonstrate that judgment and contempt have no place in our lives, because one day each of us will stand before God and "give an account of himself to God" (verse 12). Always remember this kind of judgment belongs to the Lord.

THE BOUNDARIES OF FREEDOM IN CHRIST

I mentioned earlier that I'm a father of three young children. Around our house, we take certain precautions to ensure their safety. For example, not a single electrical outlet is uncovered. Our cabinets have safety latches so the kids can't open them and take shots of cleaning solution. And all of their cups have lids so they don't wear more milk than they drink. Of course, we take these measures because our kids are young and ignorant of what would happen if they put their finger in an electrical outlet, drank cleaning fluid, or turned a cup completely vertical when drinking from it. They're young and need clear boundaries set for their own protection. However, if we're still covering outlets and putting tops on cups when they are teenagers, then we'll have a major problem. The boundaries don't just suddenly change or disappear, but our kids will eventually know where the boundaries are and what happens if ignored.

The idea of understanding boundaries—particularly when we are early in our Christian journey—reminds me of my friend's little girl, Ali, and her dance class. When Ali was five and six, the instructor would put tape on the floor so Ali would know where to step and where not to step. This helped her understand the art form and how to make dance look beautiful and keep in step with the choreography. Without the tape, Ali and her fellow dancers would move all over the stage chaotically. But as Ali ages, the instructor can remove the tape because Ali will know where to step and how to dance in a way that would make the choreographer proud.

We might not like to hear it, but we need boundaries. And early in our walk of faith, we need them as clear as tape on the floor.

Of course, boundaries aren't the goal of Christianity any more than tape on the floor is the goal of dancing. But boundaries will serve us well if we let them. Boundaries actually help us experience our freedom, as intended by the One who created freedom in the first place.

In the next section of Romans 14, Paul is going to put the tape on the floor for us. The very concept of boundaries provides enough argument to dispel the idea that our freedom is what we choose it to be. Instead, freedom is what God defines it to be. It begins with freedom from sin and freedom in Christ. In Romans 14:13-23, Paul explored the outward boundaries to our freedom as believers. While these boundaries are applicable to all in the faith, we need to remember that the strong have an extra measure of responsibility.

Don't Judge

Paul stated the first boundary as, "Let us not pass judgment on one another any longer" (Romans 14:13). The term for *judgment* focuses on criticizing and condemning. It's important to remember that even a weaker believer is still a believer, one of God's elect. The strong in faith are not to judge but to build up, not to scold but to serve, not to condemn but to carry. Gossipping about fellow Christians could also fall under this idea because it involves language that is both critical and condemning. Of all the cautions and boundaries yet to be discussed, this one may destroy community quicker than any other. We are _not_ free to say whatever we want about others.

Do Not Cause Others to Stumble

Next, the apostle Paul told believers to make a resolution with their lives not to cause another to fall into sin and warned believers not to be an obstacle that could cause fellow believers to stumble or fall: "Let us . . . decide never to put a stumbling block or hindrance in the way of a brother" (Romans 14:13). The second half of verse 13 could be translated "but rather make this your judgment, not to place a stumbling block or a deathtrap for your brother."[6]

The words *stumbling block* and *deathtrap* aren't simply synonymous with each other. A stumbling block is just what you might picture. It refers to the result of an obstacle causing someone to stumble and fall and hurt himself. The word *deathtrap* speaks of much more severe and lasting consequences. While someone might recover from a stumble, getting only a spiritual scrape of the knee, a deathtrap causes someone to fall in such a way that he or she does not recover.

While these terms are used metaphorically, there can be serious and lasting consequences from causing someone to fall into sin. The great reformer Martin Luther discussed these consequences:

> It is better to give way a little to the weak in faith until they become stronger than to have the teaching of the gospel perish completely. This work is a particularly necessary work

of love especially now when people, by eating meat and by other freedoms, are brashly, boldly and unnecessarily shaking weak consciences which have not yet come to know the truth.[7]

Don't Go Against Your Conscience

The Lord had convinced Paul that "nothing is unclean in itself" (Romans 14:14). Yet if someone believes something is unclean for him or her, then it is. Here, Paul was concerned with the weaker believer's conscience. By *unclean*, the apostle was referring to anything that was "common" and not connected to the worship and service of God.[8] Paul was not saying that sin is a matter of personal opinion, so we must be careful not to generalize this idea. He was simply expressing that certain actions in life are a matter of conscience.

Paul, who identified himself with the stronger believers, demonstrated a principle relating to the gray issues of life. As believers, we can't simply remain neutral even on issues that are a matter of opinion, because all that we do should be done for the glory of God. In other words, you can actually be in the right yet still be wrong if your attitude is messed up. Concerning these areas we've already referred to as secondary issues, whether or not they are sin comes down to a matter of your conscience. However, we need to remember that freedom in Christ is not to be abused or used to justify ungodly behavior, because that doesn't glorify God either.

Don't Prohibit Community with Fellow Believers

A community of believers is held together by love for God and love for each other. When love is violated, the community is disrupted. When Paul stated, "If your brother is grieved by what you eat, you are no longer walking in love" (Romans 14:15), he was calling for community, even though he didn't specifically use that word. If we cause fellow believers to be distressed over trivial issues, then we aren't walking in love and holding together the community of believers. Simply put, selfishness has no place in our freedom.

To grieve a fellow believer because of your personal preferences means that you have ceased to operate in love for God and others. You should always question whether or not a decision is a spiritual hindrance to another Christian. As we've seen throughout this text, freedom motivates servant-mindedness rather than self-centeredness.

Paul communicated two consequences of not walking in love: (1) fellow Christians could be grieved or hurt, and (2) they could be spiritually ruined.

Let's turn our attention to what the apostle meant by the phrase "if your brother is grieved." The example that Paul outlined in the opening verses of Romans 14 and referred to throughout the chapter has to do with an unrestricted diet. Paul probably used this issue because it was secondary and minor, which means that these principles apply to all non-primary issues. He emphasized that as believers, we must consider the effect a decision might have on our fellow believers. Freedom should never hurt or grieve others. The term for *grieve* can mean physical pain, but in this context it's more about sorrowing or distressing another's spirit.[9] In other words, turning trivial issues into primary issues can instill defeat in someone else. Paul used language just as strong in another letter where he wrote:

Food will not commend us to God. We are no worse off if we do not eat, and no better off if we do. But take care that this right [*freedom or liberty*] of yours does not somehow become a stumbling block to the weak. For if anyone sees you who have knowledge eating in an idol's temple, will he not be encouraged, if his conscience is weak, to eat food offered to idols? And so by your knowledge this weak person is destroyed, the brother for whom Christ died. Thus, sinning against your brother and wounding their conscience when it is weak, you sin against Christ. Therefore, if food makes my brothers stumble, I will never eat meat, lest I make my brother stumble. (1 Corinthians 8:8-13)

Paul then took the idea of causing other believers to stumble a step further by stating, "By what you eat, do not destroy the one for whom Christ died" (Romans 14:15). While the word *destroy* is often used in the New Testament to speak of eternal damnation, it's not limited to this concept. *Destroy* can also apply to anything that would have a destructive effect, even if it isn't final destruction itself.[10] This is the same meaning intended in Romans 14:13 with the word *deathtrap*. Paul placed a theological exclamation point at the end of 1 Corinthians 8:15, explaining that a fellow Christian for whom Christ died is not to be destroyed over something insignificant. Thus, self-centeredness or a sense of entitlement can have a devastating and lifelong damaging effect on other believers.

Don't Destroy Your Reputation

In Romans 14:16 Paul wanted to emphasize the idea that strong believers should not encourage confusion by allowing what they consider to be permissible to become food for gossip.[11] The last part of the verse has been translated "be spoken of as evil" or "be blasphemed." We should always be careful not to give the lost world any reason to make sport of Christianity or to lose sight of the true missionary cause of the church. Paul described the negative effects that occur, both inside and outside the faith, when believers misuse freedom. Not only does the body suffer, but those outside the faith will hear and believe things about Christianity that are untrue.

The reputation of the church is largely determined by how Christians treat each other. In early church history, followers of Jesus were put to death for their beliefs. No matter what else people thought, the church was known for at least one thing: their love and care for each other. Maybe you've heard that reputation takes time to build but only a moment to destroy. The church isn't perfect because those who make up the church are not perfect. However, we need to be known as people who extend grace and love to each other. My good friend David Nasser, who came to Christ from a Muslim background and now speaks to almost a million students a year, said it best: "Love is a magnet." As the church, we should have a contagious or magnetic quality about us because we have a reputation of love.

Don't Miss the Big Picture of God's Kingdom

In Romans 14:17-19, Paul shared the big picture for the Christians in the Roman church—and for us. He started by defining what the kingdom of God is (and what it is not). First, "the kingdom of God is not a matter of eating and drinking" (verse 17). This provides the basis of Paul's argument, because the kingdom of God doesn't consist of the outward things, such as meat or drink, and we should never attempt to pervert the gospel by reducing it to such trivial issues.

The nucleus of Paul's discussion on freedom always seems to find its way back to *being* as a gateway to *doing*. Being must be understood in order to see the big picture. The kingdom of God isn't understood by outward actions, but by an inward reality. As Bible teacher Warren Wiersbe noted, God's kingdom is "not the externals, but the eternals."[12] Paul then defined what these eternal, unselfish, and spiritual things are: "righteousness and peace and joy in the Holy Spirit" (verse 17).

Once we direct our attention to the eternal, we must discipline ourselves to pursue that which has eternal significance. Our freedom isn't about what we can get away with; rather, it helps us to focus on the important and to capture the moments of life. The Lord allows us to play a unique role in the epic journey called our future. Paul wrote in verse 19, "So then let us pursue what makes for peace and for mutual upbuilding." The word *pursue* carries with it the idea of going after something with earnestness and diligence in order to obtain.[13] Our success can be measured by a perspective on and obedience of eternal things. Paul challenged believers to strive after selfless spiritual things and to make peace and building up others our goal.

Don't Allow Pettiness to Destroy God's Work

Jay Strack, president and founder of Student Leadership University, told a compelling story that relates to Romans 14:20-21 in a presentation on how to manage today while creating the future. While speaking and training in San Diego, he followed an interesting news story of ten whales who beached themselves on the Baja peninsula. SeaWorld in San Diego led rescue efforts, and every radio and television station broadcast updates throughout the day on the fates of these gentle giants. Thousands of volunteers arrived on the scene anxious to help. Jay told of hearing these fatal words, delivered later the same evening: "Giants perish while chasing minnows." Part of the tragedy was that out of the nine whales that died, eight were just following the first, which was chasing the baitfish too close to the shore.

The idea of Romans 14:20 is that strong believers are never to tear down the spiritual work of God by focusing on such trivial things as food. Or you could say that those who are in Christ should not destroy what God is doing in others by chasing after the insignificant. If they do, strong believers beach themselves on the banks of pettiness and entitlement, leading those they influence down the same destructive path. The term Paul used for *tear down* or *destroy* has an opposite meaning to the word *upbuilding* or *edify*, which he used in the previous verse.

Paul went on to write, "Everything is indeed clean, but it is wrong for anyone to make another stumble by what he eats" (verse 20). This statement speaks to knowledge and intentionality. Simply put, don't do something that would cause another to stumble. We are responsible for the knowledge that we have. If we know something is offensive and still do it, then that is sinful. This text provides a serious warning for strong Christians not to chase after petty minnows because the consequences are devastating to self and others.

Don't Become Your Own Worst Enemy

In the closing verses of Romans 14, Paul warned how a Christian can be his own worst enemy. The concept of verses 22-23 deals with our personal relationship with the Lord and whether we operate by faith in whatever we do. Verse 22 is obviously directed to strong Christians, those who understand their freedom, while verse 23 is directed to weak Christians, because it speaks to those who may have doubts about what is permissible to eat. Paul encouraged the strong to enjoy and celebrate their freedom privately but not to flaunt what others might not have, because such actions could lead to judgment. When Paul stated, "Blessed is the one who has no reason to pass judgment on himself" (verse 22), he was describing someone who doesn't consciously do wrong with his freedom. This principle could be stated: Don't conduct yourself within your freedom in spite of who might be watching, but instead be sensitive to those around in light of their spiritually weaker situation.

The message of verse 23 is that operating in doubt and confusion is sin.[14] In short, if you doubt, don't do it. Why? Because God has called us to a life of faith, and faith can't exist where there is doubt. While those strong in their faith can commit sin by causing the weak to go against their conscience, the weak can commit sin by going against their own conscience. Whether strong or weak, we can be our own worst enemy.

THE OUTCOME OF FREEDOM UNDERSTOOD IS THE ATTITUDE OF CHRIST

The apostle Paul didn't end his description of freedom with the closing of Romans 14. He took his teaching on freedom in Christ to another level by using the example of Jesus in Romans 15. Jesus is the "true light" (John 1:9), and in his life we can see with high-definition clarity the attitude that can be true of all who exercise their freedom for the glory of God.

In your quest to understand freedom, I hope that your desire is to represent God well. Others may very well be drawn to the grace of God they witness in our lives along the journey to freedom. When this happens, the attitude of Christ is in us and leads us to service, community, and worship. Let's look at each of those briefly.

The Attitude of Christ in Us Produces Service

Romans 15:1 offers great insight on what a servant should look like and what service is: "We who are strong have an obligation to bear with the failings [burdens] of the weak, and not to please ourselves."

First, Paul specifically addressed those like him who are strong in the faith. He reminded them that while they aren't obligated to follow dietary customs or special days, they are not free from obligation altogether. In fact, they have an obligation to love, which is the divine "ought to" of all believers. Christians are to "bear one another's burdens" (Galatians 6:2).

The strong are to bear the weaknesses or infirmities of weak believers. Martin Luther declared, "We must not cast [the weak] aside but must bear with them until they become better. That is the way Christ treated us and still treats us every day; he puts up with our vices, our wicked morals and all our imperfection, and he helps us ceaselessly."[15]

Paul then defined *service* in the simplest of terms, noting that it means pleasing others as opposed to pleasing self.

The Attitude of Christ in Us Produces Community

Serving others is an essential element in the DNA of community. If we don't understand our freedom correctly, then we can never be rightly related to others. In Romans 15:2, 5, and 7, Paul placed a special emphasis on how freedom should lead believers to a greater sense of community. In these verses, we find certain characteristics that are necessary for community.

The first characteristic deals with the edification of our neighbors. Of course, we might logically ask, "Just who is my neighbor?" Paul seemed to be speaking of both believers and nonbelievers. We can find evidence of this in several parallel texts. Writing in the context of Christian freedom, Paul stated in 1 Corinthians 10:32-33, "Give no offense to Jews or to Greeks or to the church of God, just as I try to please everyone in everything I do, not seeking my own advantage, but that of many, that they may be saved." The idea here is that followers of Christ should serve Christians and non-Christians alike.[16] In 1 Corinthians 10:24, Paul stated, "Let no one seek his own good, but the good of his neighbor."[17] Probably the best understanding of the term *neighbor* is found in Luke 10:25-37, in the account of Jesus telling the story of the Good Samaritan. In response to the lawyer's question about who his neighbor was, Jesus demonstrated in story fashion that our neighbor is all of humanity. The big idea of that very famous story is that Jesus was about to get in the ditch with humanity and rescue them. So Paul commended strong believers to please or serve their neighbors in a way that mirrors Christ and leads to their edification. This means that those strong in the faith should serve those who don't know Christ in a way that leads to their salvation.

And the strong should also serve weaker believers in ways that help them develop into more mature Christians.[18]

Romans 15:5 provides the second characteristic of a community: like-mindedness. Verse 4 offers the key to being like-minded: "For whatever was written in former days was written for our instruction, that through endurance and through the encouragement of the Scriptures we might have hope." Like-mindedness — or what we might call harmony — can't exist if a community of believers doesn't study the Scriptures together. Paul called for a harmonious concentration on godly things. He desired a unity of perspective in that the focus of the community should be on knowing God and enjoying him together.

Verse 7 reveals the third characteristic of community: "Welcome one another as Christ has welcomed you, for the glory of God." The apostle Paul has made this appeal throughout this text; whether Jew or Gentile, weak or strong, followers of Jesus should experience a common fellowship in spite of any differences, because there is only one Christ. This common fellowship should exist based on the fact that Christ allowed man to fellowship with him. The word *welcome* can also be translated "receive" and can mean "granting someone access to your heart." This infers a much deeper fellowship and sense of community than a casual relationship. The text also speaks of an inclusive type of fellowship of both weak and strong believers. Therefore, Christ's attitude toward sinners serves as an example to believers and should inspire our focus and attitude to be the kind that naturally results in community.

The Attitude of Christ in Us Produces Worship

Personal worship is another result that we'll see when we mirror the attitude of Christ. A better understanding of personal worship contributes significantly to how we relate to fellow believers. Woven throughout Paul's teaching, especially in Romans 15:6-13, is the language of worship done corporately by the community:

- "That together you may with one voice glorify the God and Father of our Lord Jesus Christ" (verse 6).

- "Welcome one another as Christ has welcomed you, for the glory of God" (verse 7).
- "That the Gentiles might glorify God for his mercy" (verse 9).

Paul then quoted from different parts of the Old Testament (2 Samuel 22:50; Psalm 18:49; Deuteronomy 32:43; Psalm 117:1; Isaiah 11:10) to make his case that what God seeks from both the Jews and the Gentiles can be summed up with one word: worship.[19] Our freedom in Christ should serve as motivation for both private and corporate worship. Where worship is hindered, it could possibly be attributed to an abuse or misunderstanding of freedom. Christian freedom leads to a mutual praise that focuses on the redemptive work of God.

Strong believers—those enjoying their freedom without hindering their weaker brothers and sisters in the faith—aren't hard to spot. Typically, they are serving, building community, and worshipping. A few years ago, I had the privilege of speaking at an event in a rural town a couple of hours outside of Atlanta, Georgia. Before arriving at the church, I drove through miles of chicken farms, and the smell is something I will never forget.

Upon arrival, the pastor took me to his house so we could sit in a relaxed environment and get to know each other. Sitting in his den I noticed a family picture over the fireplace that featured him and his wife, their two kids, and two African American young men. I knew there was a story behind the photo, but I didn't want to be rude by asking. So I asked him to tell me the story of the church instead. He shared how when he arrived eight years earlier, about forty people were attending the church. As the new pastor, he believed that if they were to have an influence in the area, they would need to start on the local high school campus with the football team. After all, that was the most influential point in the small community.

The pastor went to the head football coach's office, introduced himself, and mentioned that he would love the opportunity to serve. The coach shared how every pastor in the county wanted the opportunity to be the chaplain and speak to the team; in a very dismissive way, the coach told the pastor that he had no need for one more preacher.

The pastor then said, "I didn't ask to speak. I asked to serve."

The coach told him that if he really wanted to help, he could serve two young men who helped the team but had some challenges. I doubt the coach ever anticipated what would happen next: that the pastor would actually serve these two young men as they in turn served the team.

Each week, the pastor helped them wash uniforms and fill water bottles. By the time the season was over, he hadn't preached to the team but he was beginning to earn the respect of the coach. When season two rolled around, this pastor simply picked up right where he had left off, serving. Season after season, the pastor served. From time to time, he would be asked to pray before a game. And if one of the other pastors didn't show up, he would fill in speaking to the team.

Sometime during the midst of all this, the aunt who took care of the two young men helping the football team came to see the pastor. She was exhausted and explained how she had taken care of them for years but didn't think she would be able to continue. In a moment of pure and undefiled religion, the pastor said he'd be happy to care for them — after all, that's what the church is supposed to be.

Fast-forward several years to me sitting in his den, wishing I could know the story behind a picture and listening to this story instead. At this point, the pastor pointed to the picture and told me that those were the two young men he had served on the football team and that they were a part of his family. After eight years, the church that previously had forty people attending now had more than eight hundred people attending. My pastor friend would tell you, as he told me, their story is one of building community through service.

That night, I met and worshipped with both of those young men. The freedom journey will lead to service that will build community and result in worship of the One who made us free.

CHAPTER 3

LIBERTY MEETS RESPONSIBILITY

Responsibility doesn't come naturally to most of us. This quality needs to be engrained into our thinking and convictions. Donald Phillips, an author who received worldwide acclaim for creating a new genre for books on historical leadership, told the story of how Abraham Lincoln came to be known as "Honest Abe."

Early in his adult life, Lincoln formed a partnership with a gentleman named William Berry to open and run a general store in New Salem, Illinois. New Salem was the kind of small town where everyone knew each other, so Lincoln's reputation for being an honest, fair, and trustworthy man spread quickly. It also made him very popular. Unfortunately, his reputation didn't save the business, but it came in handy the rest of his life. One of the reasons the store went under was because William Berry was an alcoholic. When he died in 1835, he left Lincoln with the full responsibility of repaying their acquired debt of $1,100. It would take Lincoln years to repay what he affectionately referred to as his "national debt," but he did, down to the last penny.

During this time period, the people of New Salem started calling Lincoln "Honest Abe." Years later, in 1860, the nickname "Honest Abe" was resurrected and plastered on every campaign poster. This caused many voters to see Abraham Lincoln as a man who was honest beyond question. Responsibility was the quality that served as a gateway to Lincoln's future. In addition, it is still one of the most enduring parts of his life and reputation.[1]

Responsibility is rarely convenient and almost always difficult. But to those of us who follow Christ, responsibility is an essential part of understanding freedom. Just as it defined the life of Lincoln, it should also characterize every decision we make under the umbrella of freedom. What we'll discover is that responsibility isn't in opposition or a contradiction to freedom in Christ; in fact, the opposite is true.

I sometimes tell the following story to illustrate the marriage between responsibility and freedom.

One night Liberty went to a dance. Alone she went, hoping to meet someone, hoping to fall in love. At first glance she thought, "Pickings are few!" No one caught her eye, and yet everyone was attracted to her. She couldn't move anywhere without someone asking her to dance or offering to get her some punch. Annoyed at the fact she wasn't attracted to anyone and everyone was attracted to her, she almost gave up and went home. Then, as she was heading for the door, she spotted a young man confidently leaning against the jukebox drinking punch. She wouldn't approach him, as it wasn't her style to do so. But he made his way to where she was, extended his hand, and asked if he could have this dance.

For the first time that evening, she was bashful and shy. But she extended her hand with a nervous excitement and began an adventure that could only have been created in the mind and heart of God. They danced slow songs and fast songs, drank punch and ate cake, laughed together and cried together. They never even noticed all of the other individuals beginning to leave that night. Soon they were the only ones left on the dance floor. Whatever became of Liberty and the young man she danced with named Responsibility? Soon they married and spent the rest of their days dancing harmoniously through life.

The freedom that God has given believers isn't in contradiction with responsibility. Rather, when rightly understood, the two complement each other. They flow together hand in glove like a well-choreographed dance. As in the story, everyone seems to be attracted to liberty, and many are quick to throw certain ideas and actions under her banner. The sad reality is that freedom may be the most misunderstood idea that believers celebrate because *with the sacred gift of freedom comes the weight of responsibility.* This is what the apostle Paul addressed in 1 Corinthians 10.

A RECURRING THEME

As Paul wrote of freedom in Christ in 1 Corinthians 10, his recurring theme involves doing what is best for others. Of course, this flies in the face of an "anything goes as long as it is permissible" attitude.

Eugene Peterson boldly paraphrases 1 Corinthians 10:23-24 this way in *The Message*:

> Looking at it one way, you could say, "Anything goes. Because of God's immense generosity and grace, we don't have to dissect and scrutinize every action to see if it will pass muster." But the point is not to just get by. We want to live well, but our foremost efforts should be to help others live well.

Paul seemed to filter any freedom discussion through a singular focus of serving. He stated twice in verse 23 that "all things are lawful." He also made the same statement in 1 Corinthians 6:12, where he addressed the issue of Christian freedom. Paul was teaching that mature believers learn to balance freedom and responsibility. Just because all things are lawful doesn't mean all things should be done. In other words, just because you could doesn't mean you should.

"All things are lawful" was the Corinthian slogan when it came to the issue of rights. For the Corinthians, this term meant the right to act in freedom as they saw fit or any way that felt natural. However, Paul turned that idea on its head and saw it as the right to become a servant to all so that others can be built up. It's your choice whether or not you're willing to put others ahead of your rights. Paul added a *but* to the Corinthian slogan: "'All things are lawful,' but not all things build up." The phrase *build up* is also used when describing the construction of a building, such as a house or temple. Paul's metaphorical use of this term applies to the spiritual growth of believers.

In 1 Corinthians 10:24, Paul shared that building up is for the good of one's neighbor. This is the same subject, attitude, and very similar wording that Paul used in Romans 14 and 15. In addition, Paul

building up someone else strengthens me, my faith 47

championed this idea in Philippians 2:3-4: "Do nothing from rivalry or conceit, but in humility count others more significant than yourselves. Let each of you look not only to his own interests, but also to the interests of others." Paul repeated this law of love throughout his letters because serving the interests of others goes against our nature. Thus, 1 Corinthians 10:24 is really his interpretation of freedom. He knew the Corinthians spoke much about it but didn't really understand it. Responsible freedom is prompted and governed by love, and the result is to focus on helping and building up others.

John Wesley was one of the greatest leaders of church history. In fact, in a bit you'll see that he is one of my favorite characters in all of history. Wesley preached more than 44,000 times and traveled more than 200,000 miles by horseback and carriage during his more than fifty years of ministry. He personally influenced more than 1,500 pastors and some 550 evangelists. He wrote commentaries on the Bible; a dictionary of the English language; several volumes on philosophy; several volumes on church history; a book on the history of England and Rome; books on studying Latin, Hebrew, Greek, English, and French; a few volumes on medicine; several volumes on church music; and seven volumes of sermons and papers. He was an influencer of influencers and seemed intent on rolling until the wheels fell off, even into the later years of his life—his late eighties. Methodism historians have ranked the significance of what John Wesley accomplished with his life as equal to the French Revolution and the Industrial Revolution. He was a giant and yet viewed his life through the lens of service and the building up of others. In fact, he is known for his *Rule*, which served as a filter for all of the accomplishments of his life:

Do all the good you can,
By all the means you can,
In all the ways you can,
In all the places you can,
At all the times you can,
To all the people you can,
As long as ever you can.[2]

This is the same attitude and recurring theme that continually rises to the surface throughout the apostle Paul's writings on the subject of freedom.

REAL-LIFE SCENARIOS AND THE APPLICATION OF FREEDOM

Using the example of meat sacrificed to idols, which was a very prominent issue for the believers in the Corinthian church, Paul next applied the principles in 1 Corinthians 10:23-24 to three possible scenarios that could have taken place in Corinth.

Corinth was an old city that had been rebuilt and given a new-car smell just forty to fifty years before the birth of Christ. The city was strategically placed to be a link for everyone traveling from the east to Rome, which was essentially the capital city of the world. Corinth was also a city built on the backs of slaves from many nations. Because of its location, merchants from all over the world passed through. The city had a multicultural influence that shaped it. With different cultures came different religions, many of which sacrificed animals to their idols or gods. Some of this meat would find its way into the market and onto dinner tables, and the believers in Corinth struggled with whether or not it was okay to eat this meat.

In fact, their struggle brings up a pertinent question that applies to our culture today. How should our freedom motivate and guide us through a culture littered with idolatry? Many Christians simply run from this question, because the world we navigate daily is caught up in widespread worship of things other than God.

Paul addressed the struggle faced by the Christians in Corinth — and, in turn, answers the question we face — by offering the following three scenarios to provide clarity in the midst of potentially confusing circumstances.

Scenario One: A Trip to the Grocery Store

The first scenario, which Paul addressed in 1 Corinthians 10:25-26, has to do with eating meat sold in the market, the equivalent to our modern-day grocery store. Eugene Peterson words these verses as follows in *The Message*: "Eat anything sold at the butcher shop, for instance; you don't have to run an 'idolatry test' on every item. 'The earth,' after all, 'is God's, and everything in it.' That 'everything' certainly includes the leg of lamb in the butcher shop." Other translations use the term "meat market." The original Greek term refers to a marketplace that sold meats and fish and all kinds of provisions.[3] The format of the market was a rectangular enclosed court with pillared walkways and booths on all sides.[4] The significance of referring to this type of marketplace is that there would inevitably be meat for sale that had been sacrificed to idols.

Paul was addressing the issues of conscience and freedom. Just because someone might unknowingly purchase meat that had been sacrificed to an idol didn't mean he or she was paying homage to a graven image. Paul even went so far as to instruct the Christians in Corinth not to ask any questions or run an "idolatry test" for conscience's sake. This means that the conscience should be left out of the matter. His support for this idea is a reference to Psalm 24:1: "The earth is the Lord's, and the fullness thereof." Since the earth and all that fills it is the Lord's, then basically he is in charge.

The principle that we can draw from this first scenario is that we aren't responsible for knowledge we don't have. For example, if you buy a product from a company that donates to other organizations you don't approve of, you're not responsible for the organization's actions. For example, if you buy a hamburger from a restaurant chain that in turn supports gay rights or gives to abortion clinics, and you didn't know they were doing so, you have done nothing wrong. Paul wasn't providing us with a license to be oblivious; rather, he was simply saying that we do not have to chain down our freedom because of the unknown.

Scenario Two: The Un-Rude Dinner Guest

The second scenario, in 1 Corinthians 10:27, focuses on a Corinthian Christian who is invited to dinner by an unbeliever. Paul wrote, "If one of the unbelievers invites you to dinner and you are disposed to go, eat whatever is set before you without raising any question on the ground of conscience." In short, Paul stated, if you want to go, then go and eat what is served. In fact, this type of social contact might be essential if we're to be effective at the task of sharing the gospel.[5] If no one is offended or spiritually hurt, then we have no reason to limit our freedom. We should sit, eat, enjoy, and have a Christlike perspective on the unbeliever sitting across the table with the hope that the conversation over the meal will lead that person closer to crossing the line of faith.

Reading the scenario in this verse almost sounds contradictory to the concept of responsibility. Is it really responsible to eat a leg of lamb sacrificed to a pagan god that represents the most detestable of ideas? Your personality might drive you to know everything, and when you can't know all the details, you don't get involved. Yet Paul said that when it comes to such debatable issues, relationship is more important than knowledge.

A few years ago I was in Africa preaching and serving villages with the gospel message in partnership with local churches. One day, our team gathered and drove through two hours of bush and fields. Upon our arrival at a remote village, we were welcomed by more than two hundred people singing and dancing in celebration. Soon the crowd filed into the church, where the pastor and village chief welcomed us and then invited me to preach.

After the message, we were invited to sit down, and the pastor explained that his people had prepared something special for us. A large bowl filled with rice and chunks of meat was brought in. I looked at my interpreters and asked what we should do, given that the entire church was sitting and watching us. They both smiled and said, "Eat." I looked down at the bowl of rice and meat, which had flies crawling all over it, scooped up a handful to my mouth, and smiled in gratitude.

What if that meat had been killed the night before in a ritual to false gods—a real possibility? As in the first scenario, we're responsible for the knowledge we have. As I sat in the front of that church, the goal wasn't debating such issues. Rather, the goal was building relationships and proclaiming the gospel message.

What does this look like in Western culture? Let's say a family outside the Christian faith invites you to their house for a meal. While there, make the evening about cultivating a healthy relationship. Get to know them and eat what they put in front of you. Don't go into the house with a detective's mind-set, evaluating everything in the house as you proceed forward. You're not there to be an inspector, but a friend. You're not there in the name of debatable issues, but in the name of Jesus—whether or not your hosts know it—so represent him well and just "eat."

Scenario Three: Responsible Without Being Paranoid

Paul presented the third scenario in 1 Corinthians 10:28-30:

> But if someone says to you, "This has been offered in sacrifice," then do not eat it, for the sake of the one who informed you, and for the sake of conscience—I do not mean your conscience, but his. For why should my liberty be determined by someone else's conscience? If I partake with thankfulness, why am I denounced because of that for which I give thanks?

The use of the word *someone* here could apply to either an unbeliever or someone weaker in faith. The discussion in this text has to do with the use of freedom in relation mostly to weaker believers, but also to pagans. At a festival, it might be possible that one who is a pagan or a weaker brother could provide information that the meat on the table has been sacrificed to idols. If this declaration is made, then responsible freedom requires abstinence for the sake of the conscience of the one who provided the information. The idea here is not to offend, but to stand.

When Paul asked, "Why should my liberty be determined by someone else's conscience?" he was staying consistent with his overall approach to Christian freedom. He had every *right* to sit at that table and eat meat with the individual making this statement. However, he knew the issue wasn't just a matter of rights but also what was wise for him to do. When we know what's wise but don't do it, we sin, because we're unconcerned about the spiritual well-being of others.

Of course, this doesn't mean Paul was going to walk around on eggshells, constantly held hostage by what some could possibly think! He would eat what's served and be grateful to the Lord who provided it. This is the perspective he gave when he asked, "If I partake with thankfulness, why am I denounced because of that for which I give thanks?" (verse 30).

So what are we to make of Paul's teaching, particularly given that the apostle seems to move from eating to not eating to eating in these few short verses? We must conclude that we're responsible for the knowledge we have no matter what scenario we find ourselves in. Knowing demands a degree of responsibility to others who might be watching.

THE GOAL OF RESPONSIBLE FREEDOM: TO GLORIFY GOD EXHAUSTIVELY

Responsible freedom—even when motivated by others who might be observing our actions—is ultimately responsible only to God. Paul wrote in 1 Corinthians 10:31: "So, whether you eat or drink, or whatever you do, do all to the glory of God."

This naturally causes us to ask, *What actions bring glory to God?* Start with this: If an action is inconsistent with what the Bible teaches elsewhere concerning freedom in Christ, then that action doesn't bring glory to God. The Greek word for *glory* is defined as "a public manifestation of an inner reality."[6] Responsible freedom means that all actions are done in light of the great reality that we are new creations in Christ. We should always be conscious of how we're living out our freedom. In other words, we need more than just good intentions to glorify God. Bringing him glory involves right motives that lead to righteous actions.

Paul reminded us how we can bring God glory when he urged believers, by the mercies of God, to present their bodies as a living sacrifice (see Romans 12:1). When we understand the phrase *living sacrifice*, we begin to understand what it means to do all for the glory of God.

Because of the time and audience of Paul's letters, a sacrifice would have been understood to be an animal, maybe a lamb or a calf, which had been raised for the distinct purpose of being sacrificed in a temple by a priest. In the same way, a follower of God is to live as if the purpose for his entire existence is for the present moment. As living sacrifices we should seek to capture each moment of life to the glory of God as if that moment were the last opportunity we'd have to do so. After reading 1 Corinthians 10:31, we should ask, "Do I capture the moments of life?" I've heard it said, "There are only two days in life that matter: this day and that day." *This* day is the day that is presently at hand. *That* day would be the day we stand before the Lord and give an account of our lives.

Note how Paul addressed what actions we should do to the glory of God: "Whether you eat or drink, or whatever you do." Paul stepped outside the meat-to-idols example and applied this general principle to any action we might take. One scholar put it this way: "When we eat or drink, drive our car, do our work with energy, or relax by playing a game, most of the time we are not thinking about God while we are acting. But everything in our lives must certainly fit within a program whose goal is the glory of God."[7]

A few years ago a close friend of mine, Alan, fell into the prison of addiction. Within a short amount of time he succumbed to the alcoholism that had tortured him prior to his salvation. He was under a lot of stress and a busy schedule. Then one night on a plane, the flight attendant offered him a drink before takeoff. One wasn't enough and one was too many.

Alan's drinking went on for some time before it came to the attention of some godly men who loved him and cared for his soul. He agreed with them that he needed help, and they began to research rehabilitation facilities. By divine providence they drove him through the night to a facility a few hundred miles away. Upon arrival, they realized it wasn't all the website had described. The buildings sat in the middle of hundreds of acres of woods and rows of corn, there was no air conditioning or television, and his room was just a bed surrounded by rough cinder blocks. Alan is an educated man who had spoken to many large crowds and led a successful organization. But the individuals in this facility were there because it was free and the only one they could afford.

When Alan went inside the main building, he walked over and sat down at a table of guys listening to a required Bible study. The gentleman sitting next to him couldn't read or write, and he was missing most of his teeth. This was representative of the entire group. The men who had driven Alan to this facility immediately said this wasn't the place for him and they would take him to a much nicer rehabilitation center. But Alan told them he was where he needed to be and would see them in two months.

Every day, Alan had one of two tasks: cut grass or harvest corn. Yes, he also attended Bible study and church, but working the fields consumed most of his time. He recalls pushing a lawn mower in one-hundred-degree heat fifty yards one way, only to turn around and push it fifty yards the other way for hour after hour. One day, while pushing that mower and reflecting on his life and how he would one day again do something that glorified God, Alan realized that he was glorifying God in that moment. He found himself at perfect peace alone with God in that field cutting grass.

Alan's experience taught me something powerful about the Christian life: Glorifying God isn't about the size of your actions or the significance of your successes; rather it's about the surrender of your heart. This is what it means to capture the moments and be intentional about choosing freedom daily.

To Glorify God Motivates a Proactive Selflessness Toward Humanity

While you can offend someone without meaning to, the majority of the time we offend others because of a self-centered attitude. I remember early in my marriage, my wife and I had some friends over for dinner and a movie. A new movie had just come out that I really wanted to see — you know the kind where the plot takes a backseat to explosions and gunfights every five minutes! In addition to the gratuitous violence and unrealistic weaponry, the movie also contained some disturbing language that I would have known about if I had done my homework. As everyone piled into the den and the movie began, I noticed that one of my friends quietly left our home. Later, I learned that he'd made a commitment not to watch movies with certain curse words in them. I would have known that if I hadn't been so selfish and at least cared enough to ask if this particular movie might offend anyone.

In 1 Corinthians 10:32, the apostle Paul said to "give no offense to Jews or to Greeks or to the church of God." Paul was addressing how to do all to the glory of God. God is glorified when believers are living free, with a clear conscious, and causing no offense but rather building up the body of Christ. In this one verse Paul mentioned Jews, Greeks, and the church. This description includes people who the Corinthian Christians might have agreed or strongly disagreed with, those who were enemies of Christianity or indifferent altogether toward spiritual things, and fellow church members. To give no reason for them to stumble is a proactive selfless act.

To Glorify God Motivates Us to Lead Others to Salvation

Paul next provided a hopeful conclusion to living out our duty of responsible freedom — namely, the salvation of the lost. He used himself as an example, saying, "Just as I try to please everyone in everything I do, not seeking my own advantage, but that of many, that they may be saved" (1 Corinthians 10:33). He expounded on this idea earlier in 1 Corinthians 9:19-25 where he summed it all up saying, "For though I am free from all, I have made myself a servant to all, that I might win more of them" (verse 19). In both of these texts, Paul emphasized that those things that enabled him to do the most for the cause of Christ determined the outward works of his faith.

The thread of selflessness is intrinsically woven through Christian freedom as a reflection of the love of God. As he sought to build the church and win the lost, Paul wasn't seeking his own profit; he was a servant of God and thus a servant of humanity. In the end, out of all of God's creation, the only thing that will last forever is people. Paul had more than a casual understanding of this, which motivated him to glorify God as he sought to have influence that would reap eternal results. Responsible freedom binds a holy obligation "both to Greeks and to barbarians, both to the wise and to the foolish" (Romans 1:14, NASB).

Years ago when I was in high school, I had a neighbor named Jesse. He was an underclassman, and I didn't want to be interrupted by getting to know him (it wasn't until later in life that I realized the mind games we play in high school are futile and can have lasting consequences). I never spoke to Jesse even though I always saw him driving his four-wheeler up and down the gravel-dirt road by our house. He must have loved that machine because I think he drove it every day. But one day, he wasn't there. I'll never forget my dad's words the day Jesse died in an accident: "I try to be a witness for the cause of Christ everywhere I go, and somehow I forgot to go next door." At that moment, I realized that I had failed to see the people living in the house next to mine as infinitely valuable.

We must understand that our freedom should motivate us to see others released from the bondages of sin, even at the risk of sounding preachy. In the end, people go to heaven and people go to hell. Those of us fortunate enough to bear his name have the sacred responsibility, in both the secondary and primary issues we wrestle with, to always be pointing people to Christ.

To Glorify God Motivates Us to Be an Example to Be Followed

Responsible freedom can be imitated and must be consistent with Christ: "Be imitators of me, as I am of Christ" (1 Corinthians 11:1). No other verse gives as much insight into Paul's character as an apostle, pastor, evangelist, and Christian than the words "imitate me." (Note that although 1 Corinthians 10 ends at verse 33, it seems — based on the flow of the argument — that the conclusion of Paul's discussion should occur with 1 Corinthians 11:1.)

The great reformer John Calvin pointed out two things to be observed in this verse: "First, that [Paul] prescribes nothing to others that he had not first practiced himself; and secondly, that he directs himself and others to Christ as the only pattern of right acting."[8] A great question to ask ourselves in a discussion on responsible freedom is "Can others imitate me, and in doing so will they mirror Christ?" Paul's words provide the answer. The goal is to "do all to the glory of God" (1 Corinthians 10:31). And this will never be more evident than when we are living a life that can be imitated.

One of my favorite characters throughout history is John Wesley, and probably not for the reason you think. Yes, he led a great movement that allowed millions to hear the gospel message. And, yes, he was also the organizational leader that paved the way for the birth of the Methodist Church. He was a man of great tenacity, who rode on horseback through swamps and storms, hot and cold, just to preach the gospel to those who needed to hear it. However, the reason I hold him in such high regard is because of his strong stance against the evil institution of slavery. At that particular time in history, slavery was accepted by most, including the church.

When Wesley was a young minister, he went on a missionary trip from England to Georgia. While in America, he traveled to other southeastern states like South Carolina, where he was introduced first-hand to the ugly reality of slavery. During this time, his convictions were strengthened, and he spent the rest of his life in opposition to the practice. For all practical purposes, Wesley stood alone on this issue. Even his close friend George Whitefield, a great minister of the gospel, believed it was acceptable to own slaves as long as they were treated humanely. In fact, Whitefield used slaves to work and build his orphanages.

At the age of eighty-eight, knowing he was days from dying, Wesley crawled out of his deathbed and wrote one final letter. The letter was addressed to none other than the young William Wilberforce, a man who would spend his life fighting to overturn slavery in England. Wesley died within a few days, without ever seeing the institution of slavery overturned. While Wilberforce had many influences and examples in his life—from the prime minister of England to the author of "Amazing Grace," John Newton—no one can dismiss the inspiration of the last letter of a dying man. In the end, God chose not to use the preacher Wesley, but the politician Wilberforce to see this task come to fruition. Wesley's life, convictions, and his stance on slavery served as an example to be followed, a life to be imitated.

This is the great challenge for us today . . . to live lives worthy of imitation. Fewer ideas are more convicting and motivating than the thought that someone could be imitating us, following us as an example. Yet, this is the goal of freedom: that in following our example, others will be led to the feet of Jesus.

CHAPTER 4

CHRIST HAS SET US FREE

As you might remember from history class, the Civil War was one
of the most crucial times in America's history. Abraham Lincoln
was the president, and he is still considered one of the greatest leaders this
world has ever had.

Lincoln had a deep-seated conviction against slavery and felt it was
both degrading and unconstitutional. His disgust was revealed in a letter
he wrote in 1855: "As a nation we began by declaring that 'all men are created equal.' We now practically read it 'all men are created equal, except
Negroes.'"[1]

Lincoln's legacy is in many ways defined by the Civil War and the
signing of the Emancipation Proclamation, which essentially freed all
slaves in states not under the control of the Union. More than 3 million
slaves in the confederate territory were freed. Of course, this decision was
unwelcomed by many southern slave owners. As the news of the proclamation spread, slave masters lied in order to keep their slaves working.
Slaves were told that the proclamation was a lie and that just as their
mothers and fathers had been slaves, they were slaves and always would
be. Believing the lie, many slaves returned to the field, giving up their
granted freedom.

Possibly the most tragic state of existence is to be free yet live in bondage. If you deny yourself the opportunity to live free once you have been
made free in Christ, you are actually denying the power of the cross of
Christ. My life managed in my own hands, or in the hands of religion, is a
disaster. But my life in the hands of Jesus is beautiful. Our great privilege
is to have our position in this life transformed from bondage to freedom
by the only One who has the authority to do so.

In Galatians 5, the apostle Paul provided some of the single greatest statements concerning freedom in Christ. In fact, the first verse is considered the Magna Carta of Christian freedom: "For freedom Christ has set us free; stand firm therefore, and do not submit again to a yoke of slavery." The grace of God and the freedom it offers seem too good to be true. The chains that once enslaved us have been taken off, and we've been *made free*! Don't go back to bondage. The slaves during the 1860s had been set free by someone who had authority to do so, yet they were told a lie and had no reason not to believe it. God has proven Himself in Jesus, and we have no reason to be in bondage to any lie from Satan.

Galatians 5:1 contains two commands. In the first, Paul used some of the strongest language in his entire letter to the Christians in Galatia: "Stand firm." Because of who God is and what He has done for us in Jesus Christ, we are to make visible in the earthly realm of our human existence what God has already declared in the divine verdict of justification.[2] As Christians, we are called to step up to the plate and fully embrace our identity in everyday comings and goings, realizing this freedom is our divine birthright.

Do you recognize the freedom that Paul wrote of here? It's not about civil liberty or carnal liberty, but freedom from the bondage of sin. In Romans 6:6-7, Paul gave the reason for this freedom: "We know that our old self was crucified with him in order that the body of sin might be brought to nothing, so that we would no longer be enslaved to sin. For one who has died has been set free from sin." Our freedom is a result of the redemptive work of Christ. Nothing is casual about the sacrificial love of Christ, so we can't take a relaxed approach to this freedom. By its very nature, sacrificial love demands an exhaustive response.

The second command in Galatians 5:1 is "do not submit again to a yoke of slavery." The word *again* indicates that we can temporarily lose or surrender our freedom if we choose to become entangled in the bondage of sin. Only God can set us free, but we who have been set free are responsible to live out our freedom through the decisions we make.

In the late 1990s, a movie was released titled *The Man in the Iron Mask*, which was set in France during the 1600s. In 1638, Queen Anne of France gave birth to a boy who was to be the next king, Louis XIV. Known only to a few, a twin was born just minutes later and immediately placed into hiding. As time passed and through an unfortunate set of circumstances, the twin was locked into an iron mask to hide his identity and placed in an obscure prison where he was to remain until the end of his life. Meanwhile, the city of Paris was starving due to the costs of war, as well as the king's interests of money and women. The famous three musketeers, now retired, formed a plot to rescue the man in the iron mask and replace King Louis with him in hopes of saving France. After an epic rescue, they took the twin to a country house for safekeeping and removal of the mask. For the first time in six years, he was given a bed to sleep in, clean clothes to wear, and good food to eat. But later in the evening, the freed man stood alone in his room with the mask back on his face.

This story illustrates what happens to so many believers: They miss out on what it means to live free. We are free, and that means we never have to wear the iron mask of bondage again. Yet some of us do. Why? Could it be that we are more comfortable in our sin? Maybe a victim mentality or a sense of entitlement causes such behavior. In any case, there are no excuses. You and I don't have to return to our sin ever again because we are free and can stand firm, deeply rooted in our faith.

In Galatians 5:2, Paul left no doubt about who is communicating with them: "Look: I, Paul, say to you." He stressed his identity because many false teachers had come to the Galatian church. The false teachers taught that the Torah, the Old Testament law, must be embraced in order to have Christian salvation.

Paul continued to give a stern warning against circumcision in verses 2-3. This practice was essential to Judaism as taught in the Torah. Circumcision can be understood literally but also symbolically as representing the entire burden of all the Jewish obligations dictated by the Torah. Paul said that to trust in circumcision — or anything you can do on your own — means that "Christ will be of no advantage to you." In other words, you can't be the servant of two masters. Trust Christ or trust religion. The Torah represents the old covenant while Christ represents the new covenant, and we must choose only one. Paul condemned, in the strongest terms, observance of the whole law because righteousness of works and justification by faith cannot coexist. John Chrysostom, who was considered the early church's greatest preacher, said, "He who is circumcised [for justification] is so as fearing the law, and he who fears, disbelieves the power of grace, and he who disbelieves can profit nothing by that grace which he disbelieves."[3]

The Message words Galatians 5:4 like this: "I suspect you would never intend this, but this is what happens. When you attempt to live by your own religious plans and projects, you are cut off from Christ, you fall out of grace." Paul was addressing faith that is used in the outward act of observing the law. One mistaken idea that people buy into is that justification can be achieved by keeping the rules. But the rules are useless in justification. The term *cut off* (or "severed") refers to someone withdrawing from Christ and not having any fellowship with Him.[4] An effort to be justified by any law undermines or sterilizes the present-day effect of living in freedom. This isn't about eternal security, but present fellowship. How miserable this must be for a believer!

Martin Luther's life offers a great illustration of this truth. Prior to the Reformation, he sought to be justified before God by punishing his body in many different ways. Later, he wrote of this verse,

If you think Christ and the Law can dwell together in your heart, you may be sure that Christ dwells not in your heart. For if Christ is in your heart He neither condemns you, nor does He ever bid you to trust in your own good works. If you know Christ at all, you know that good works do not serve unto righteousness, nor evil works unto condemnation. I do not want to withhold from good works their due praise, nor do I wish to encourage evil works. But when it comes to justification, I say, we must concentrate upon Christ alone, or else we make Him non-effective. You must choose between Christ and the righteousness of the Law. If you choose Christ you are righteous before God. If you stick to the Law, Christ is of no use to you.[5]

The final phrase in Galatians 5:4, which refers to falling from grace, indicates that if someone tried to keep the rules as the route to righteousness, there will be a fatal outcome. While modern-day Christ followers don't necessarily struggle with following the Torah or laws about circumcision, the principle is still relevant. As with Paul's original audience, many of us trust in our own morality as a means of justification. Whether it be abstaining from sexual activity or any number of vices, or the number of good deeds acquired in a lifetime such as feeding the poor and helping the elderly, we can never be good enough. Trusting in our own good works to be made righteous before God is like a man wandering in the desert toward a mirage. No matter how fast or how long he walks, he'll eventually die of thirst. Good works alone will leave us completely unsatisfied and lost; only the sufficiency of Christ can satisfy our eternal thirst.

Paul shifted gears in verse 5 and used emphatic language to set apart as true Christians himself and others from those who merely call themselves Christian. He brought together the three key words of the argument thus far: Spirit, faith, and righteousness.

The mention of the Spirit in this description of the Christian life hints at the prominent role he will play in the remainder of this discussion. The phrase "by faith" in the end of verse 5 is a key component of community and has a strong connection to "love" at the end of verse 6. In addition, believers encounter "the hope of righteousness." Altogether, these words describe the freedom that Paul presently enjoyed but are more of a preview of coming attractions because total sanctification and glorification still await him and all believers. In other words, Jesus has made us free today and free forever. To live in that freedom is not to surrender in any way to bondage and cause Christ to profit nothing; rather, to live in freedom is to enjoy the liberated life for which Christ died and to experience faith working through love. Freedom admonishes believers to drop their legalism.

Our freedom has nothing to do with human achievement and everything to do with Christ's sufficiency. And as Paul explained, the bottom line is faith (not works) expressed through love, not religious plans or projects. We can so easily fall into the trap of *doing* rather than *being* as the means for success. But we must always remember that <u>we live free</u> <u>because we are free</u>, not because we are <u>trying to earn our freedom</u>.

I believe Christ followers should be baptized following their conversion, making a public declaration that Christ is their Savior and that they are now part of the community or church. Baptism doesn't earn or complete salvation. Rather it's an act of obedience that demonstrates salvation has already taken place. It's like the wedding ring I wear so that everyone knows I belong to my wife, Christina. We wouldn't say that the ring itself is Christina any more than we'd say that baptism is salvation. Yet both are sacred symbols. A symbol accomplishes nothing; instead, it serves as a constant reminder of something that has already been accomplished. Whether it's the circumcision that Paul talked about or modern-day baptism, neither offers salvation, which is the basis for freedom.

In short, faith in Christ alone equals salvation, not Christ plus . . . well, anything.

THE BIG IDEA: CONTROLLED BY THE SPIRIT OR THE FLESH?

So far, the apostle Paul has demonstrated freedom to the Galatian believers. He wanted them to remove themselves from the slavery of the law imposed on them by the Jewish teachers. Next, he proceeded to show how liberty manifests and exercises itself in the Christian life.[6] He reminded them of the big idea in Galatians 5:13-15, starting with "For you were called to freedom, brothers."

Throughout his writings, Paul always had a way of bringing the focus back to the true issue at hand. Here, the issue is freedom, and he didn't want the Galatian Christians to lose sight of that because the result could have had disastrous consequences. John Calvin wrote, "Liberty lies in the conscience, and looks to God; the use of it lies in outward matters, and deals not with God only, but with men."[7] The big idea of liberty is not that you operate by what feels natural or that you are without a strong regulation. Nothing could be further from the truth, because we are always to be controlled by the strongest of regulators—"by love."

My freedom came by Christ's love then I should exercise my freedom with love. Love is the fuel for freedom

Paul elaborated by explaining what freedom is not. He first pointed out that freedom is not "an opportunity for the flesh" (verse 13). The term *flesh* is now the new term in Paul's argument, replacing the negative example of the law he had used up to this point. The word *flesh* speaks of weakness and the sinful nature. Paul was very careful not to paint a false picture of living on the defensive, always wondering what sin you can escape. Instead, liberty is an opportunity to live out freedom by having love dictate action—particularly the action of serving one another. Jesus provided the greatest example of this when he said, "For who is the greater, one who reclines at table or one who serves? Is it not the one who reclines at table? But I am among you as the one who serves" (Luke 22:27). Paul went so far as to say this love is how the law is fulfilled.

At this point, Paul had set up the dilemma well and transitioned with the command to "walk by the Spirit" (verse 16). Throughout the rest of Galatians 5, Paul contrasted the "spirit" and the "flesh," but first he expressed the urgency of this command. Walking in the Spirit speaks of how we conduct our daily life.[8] Clearly, Paul's only answer to victorious living or living a life of freedom is by the Holy Spirit. This command is immediately followed by a promise: If you walk by the rule of the Spirit, you will not gratify the desires of the flesh.

During my teenage years, I heard quite a few sermons from youth speakers about not having sex. Most of those presentations painted and sometimes showed actual pictures of consequences that involved STDs and death. I could only conclude that the goal of all this was to scare us into not having premarital sex or fooling around. It worked, too—at least for a little while. However, as soon as an ungodly opportunity with the opposite sex presented itself, the consequences seemed like white noise. Based on those talks, another conclusion I came to was that consequences were the central motivation of the Christian life. I felt like I'd make God happy if I just stayed out of His way and didn't get into too much trouble. But the truth is that some consequences were too small to serve as a big motivation.

One of the major roles of the Holy Spirit is to point us to Jesus. Our fleshly desires (like having premarital sex) point us away from God toward ungodliness. Ungodliness means living as if God's standards don't exist. While my flesh might want to have premarital sex, the Spirit convicts my heart and mind of truth and reminds me that I would be stepping outside of my freedom in gratifying my own desires. But if I walk in the Spirit, I am free to love God with all of my existence!

The desires of the flesh will be addressed later in Galatians 5, but for now Paul restated a principle that he put forth in Romans 13:14: "But put on the Lord Jesus Christ, and make no provision for the flesh, to gratify its desires." Galatians 5:17 speaks to how the flesh and the Spirit are diametrically opposed to one another. The word translated "opposed" or "contrary" paints the flesh and Spirit as adversaries.[9] This verse explains the reason for the command and promise in verse 16: If we walk in the Spirit, we will not carry out the desires of the flesh.

THE VICE LIST: WORKS OF THE FLESH

Freedom in Christ can't be characterized by the works of the flesh, because the works of the flesh are against the Spirit. The flesh imprisons individuals in the confines of sinful addiction. New Testament scholar Gordon Fee used the phrases "vice list" and "virtue list" to describe the works of the flesh and the works of the Spirit.[10] Paul warned in the strongest possible terms that those who practice the works of the flesh "will not inherit the kingdom of God" (Galatians 5:21). He spoke of a habitual practice of these things, which indicates the character of the individual.[11] In short, the works of the flesh do not describe those who are in Christ.

The works of the flesh are listed in Galatians 5:19-21:

> sexual immorality, impurity, sensuality, idolatry, sorcery, enmity, strife, jealousy, fits of anger, rivalries, dissensions, divisions, envy, drunkenness, orgies, and things like these. I warn you, as I warned you before, that those who do such things will not inherit the kingdom of God.

These works of the flesh can be broken down into four broad categories: *illicit sex*, which includes sexual immorality, impurity, and sensuality; *illicit worship*, which includes idolatry and sorcery; *breakdown in relationships*, which includes enmity, strife, jealousy, fits of anger, rivalries, dissensions, divisions, and envy; and *excesses*, which include drunkenness and orgies.[12] This isn't an exhaustive list; for example, lust and covetousness are missing. However, Paul did conclude with the phrase "and things like these."

This is a serious statement for all Christians in all places at all times. Christ's death has delivered believers from such vices, and the Spirit has empowered us to never surrender to our sinful nature. The majority of the list describes the type of behavior that is visible and not internal. This is a portrait of the fruit of the sinful nature. The majority of the items on the list are sins that can contribute to the breakdown of community, which seems to be a constant theme weaving its way throughout Paul's writings on freedom. Christian freedom means that as believers, we are free from the bondage of sin and from indulging in any of the works of the flesh.

Interestingly, the above vice list reads like an information guide for most of today's reality-television shows! Surrendering to the desires of the flesh can destroy our purity, our worship, our relationships, and our life. Bob Reccord, a popular conference speaker and author, told a story of how the desires of the flesh can have lasting consequences:

> It had been more than a decade since what Kathy called her wild period—six years of sexual abandon, four in college and two as a single woman living in the city. Somehow she'd managed to slip through those years without succumbing to a sexually transmitted disease or getting pregnant.
>
> But tonight Kathy lay in bed beside her sleeping husband Brad, a loving man who provided well for her and the kids—and who came home to her every night. He was snoring gently, but she was wide awake. Images of other men kept popping into her head, despite the fact that Brad was a wonderful lover. Not only images but feelings. Feelings of

guilt, shame, confusion—what she had suffered during the wild period when she sought total freedom.

And now these feelings were coming to the surface. They were crowding out the good feelings of joy and wholeness and security she should be feeling. During her wild period Kathy believed the lie that she would be able to put all this behind her when she settled down to become a faithful wife, as she eventually did. But the memories haunted her—like tonight, when love was supposed to be pure and beautiful and good.

She plumped her pillow. It would be a long night.[13]

THE VIRTUE LIST: FRUIT OF THE SPIRIT

Paul's language changed with regard to the works of the flesh and the fruit of the Spirit. While *works* puts an emphasis on human ventures, *fruit* speaks to God's divine empowerment. The fruit of the Spirit is an indication that believers are led by the Spirit and not under the law (see Galatians 5:18). The fruit being produced in believers mirrors the very character of God. Therefore, Christian freedom not only motivates but also actually cultivates the character of God in our lives.

The fruit of the Spirit is listed in Galatians 5:22-23: "love, joy, peace, patience, kindness, goodness, faithfulness, gentleness, self-control; against such things there is no law." The nineteenth-century theologian J. B. Lightfoot divided this list into three groups:

The first of these comprises Christian habits of mind in their more general aspect, "love, joy, peace"; the second gives special qualities affecting a man's interactions with his neighbor, "long-suffering, kindness, beneficence"; while the third, again general in character like the first, exhibits the principles which guide a Christian's conduct, "honesty, gentleness, temperance."[14]

These virtues stand in direct contrast to the works of the flesh. Walking in the Spirit means to live consistently with the rule of the Spirit. Of fundamental significance to freedom in Christ is evaluation of our lives as believers to see if we are living in ways consistent with the picture Paul painted here.

This is a great litmus test of whether you are living in liberty or bondage. Is your life full of fruit or weeds? What characterizes your life? Is it the fruit of the Spirit or the works of the flesh? Only you can make that decision.

This past Father's Day I received a card with a recorded voice message inside from my kids. Only having ten short seconds to record a message, my kids screamed, "I love you, Daddy!" as loud as they could over and over. It made me think, *If my life were opened up and only one short message could come out, what would that message be?* If we were to take all that we know of Paul's life from his writings, we could easily conclude that the message of his existence was grace. After all, he mentioned grace more than a hundred times in thirteen letters.

If someone were to gather all the knowledge he could from your life, what conclusion would the evidence point to? Would the message of your life be rules motivated by religious obligation or morality motivated by consequences? Or would your life be supremely motivated by grace and love?

On the heels of his discussion of the flesh and the Spirit, Paul again returned to the theme of serving others in Galatians 6. This theme has grown stronger with each passage we've studied. In fact, when we bear one another's burdens, we fulfill the law of Christ. If you are fulfilling the law of Christ — the law of love — you will serve. And when you serve, the fruit of the Spirit will be evident in your life. As Paul noted in verses 14-15, we get to observe the declaration of someone truly free in Christ:

For my part, I am going to boast about nothing but the Cross of our Master, Jesus Christ. Because of that Cross, I have been crucified in relation to the world, set free from the stifling atmosphere of pleasing others and fitting into the little patterns that they dictate. Can't you see the central issue in all this? It is not what you and I do—submit to circumcision, reject circumcision. It is what *God* is doing, and he is creating something totally new, a free life! (MSG)

CHAPTER 5

ASKING THE RIGHT QUESTIONS

W hen I was young and ignorant, I enjoyed the circus. I especially loved watching the elephants perform. The elephant is the largest of all land mammals and can survive up to seventy years in the wild. In a single day, an elephant can drink sixty-seven gallons of water and walk up to thirty miles. It's an amazing creature that has captured my imagination for years.

But have you ever seen a circus elephant when it wasn't performing under the big top? If you have, then you undoubtedly saw a stake or peg in the ground and a chain running from it to one of the elephant's hind legs. It's a sad picture for the elephant because it can go nowhere. Yet it's just a stake, and this is one of the strongest creatures on earth. With hardly any effort, it could break free from the pegged prison. Why doesn't it? Because when the elephant was just a baby, it was chained to that stake. And at that time, it didn't have the strength to break free. Somewhere along the way, the elephant gave up and accepted that being chained to a stake in the ground was reality and couldn't be changed. The adult elephant never escapes because it lives on the wrong assumption that its captivity is simply how things are.

My goal with this book is to give you a tool so that you never have to live on assumptions. God doesn't intend for us to live in captivity to the idea that "this is as good as it gets." Don't be afraid to challenge everything based on what the Bible teaches. If the Bible is absolute truth—which I hope you are convinced of—then it can handle any of life's gray or confusing issues. Assumptions confine and freedom is, well, freeing: "Trust in the LORD with all your heart and lean not on your own understanding; in all your ways acknowledge him, and he will make your paths straight" (Proverbs 3:5-6, NIV).

FREEDOM IS PART OF A BRIDGE

Thousands of years ago, the Romans built small humpbacked bridges over many streams throughout Europe. For two millennia, people and wagons safely went over them. But today, if you were to drive a heavy truck over one, it would break. It doesn't have a sufficiently strong base, and it can't withstand the pressures of something heavy.[1]

The "how to believe" grid, which we'll outline in this chapter, is much more than a tool to figure out what you can and can't do. Rather it's a foundational block upon which the bridge from this life to the next is built. It enables you to withstand the pressures and weight of the elephants in the room. Without this foundational block in our belief system, our journey becomes a lot like the two-thousand-year-old humpback bridges, completely unprepared for the pressures to come.

An old Hindu proverb states, "You can eat an elephant one bite at a time." Regardless of the fact that it's illegal in most states to kill elephants and that eating them should be a crime punishable by death, the principle remains true. We can accomplish something big by reducing it to a series of small tasks. Unfortunately, we've become a culture addicted to the quick fix. We watch movies where the hero saves the world in under two hours. TV has show after show with sitcom characters resolving mega moral issues in less than thirty minutes — twenty if you count commercials. We instantly download everything from music to recipes. It's possible to instant message someone on the other side of the world and get a response without enough time to catch a breath in between. We like things done at the speed of now and have very little patience for . . . well, anything.

There is nothing quick about defining your beliefs; instead, it's a journey. You can't download it, instant message it, hurry it, or even wait for it. You must attack it one bite at a time until nothing is left of the once-massive beast that stood before you. The bites you take out of the big elephants in your life are the right questions you ask. The process of struggling through one right question after another reduces these pachyderms down until there is nothing left and you stand convinced in your mind.

Then you can have a cookie.

The concept of freedom in Christ can't be reduced to simple informational download or intake. While the previous chapters examined and extracted great biblical realities concerning freedom — and I did try to provide some bite-sized help in how to live and enjoy that freedom — this journey will now take a much more experiential turn. We'll call upon an age-old method that Jesus utilized to help his followers navigate the issues of life: *the art of asking the right questions.*

Therefore, the purpose of this chapter is to help us chase down the elephants in our lives, set the table, and begin to eat them one bite at a time. We'll accomplish this through a set of principles in the form of questions that can help us maneuver the gray areas of life and discern the best possible decisions. These principles will enable us to identify what honors God the most by asking the right questions.

Before moving forward, we should note that no one has the right to impose or pass judgments on another's opinions in dealing with morally debatable issues (see Romans 14:3). The only option believers have is to accept one another because God has accepted us. While there are strong and weak believers, all of us have some type of spiritual baggage. The difference is that the weak believer is wed to a rule-oriented, mechanical faith,[2] while the strong believer understands and lives in freedom.

In their book *Ethics for a Brave New World*, John and Paul Feinberg summarized it this way: "If there is any judging at all, it must be done by each individual concerning himself and by Christ who judges (Romans 14:4,10-13)."[3] Remember, Paul taught that if our conscience has determined that something morally debatable or neutral is wrong for us, then it *is* wrong for us (see Romans 14:14). Therefore, "something morally neutral becomes a sin if one thinks it is wrong but does it anyway (Romans 14:22-23)."[4]

We'll now formulate into questions all of the components we've extracted from the words of Scripture we've been examining since the beginning of the book.

1. Is the Decision Within the Moral Will of God?

This first question encompasses a great deal. First, we have to determine exactly what the moral will of God is. I like the rather simple way that Garry Friesen, professor of Bible at Multnomah Bible College, defined it. He said the moral will of God is "the revealed commands in the Bible that teach how people ought to believe and live."[5] God's moral will is the expression of his character through the special revelation of the Bible. It influences every facet and moment of life, goals, attitudes, means, and perspectives and is able to equip believers for every good work.[6]

In his highly acclaimed book *Decision Making and the Will of God,* Friesen suggested three disciplines to help one know and live the moral will of God:

- Designate time to read through portions of Scripture with friends
- Have a plan to memorize Scripture so that key passages can be recalled
- Memorize short titles for every chapter in certain portions of Scripture[7]

For those of us who claim to follow Christ, one of the tragic reasons we don't understand our freedom is because we don't study the Scriptures. Therefore, we don't know what the Bible says. When dealing with a decision, the first question should always be, "Has God already dealt directly with this issue in Scripture?" Many of us don't live a liberated life because we're in bondage to laziness. Sadly, laziness is not just harmful, but it's also a gateway to an apathetic attitude.

So, before we decide on a morally neutral decision, we must first be clear that the issue is indeed morally neutral.

2. Is the Decision Being Made in the Attitude of Christ (Romans 15:1-13)?

Christ's attitude of selfless love serves as the great motivator for those who truly understand what it is to live in freedom. The apostle Paul taught in Romans 15 that when a believer mirrors the attitude of Christ, then serving, community, and worship will result. This question needs to be asked early because if we don't seek to walk in Christ (see Colossians 2:6), then we'll never reflect his attitude and we'll make selfish decisions.

Our attitude will be the single most important decision that we make each day. It's the open door to wisdom, and it positions us to make wise decisions during the journey.

3. Is the Decision Being Made Under the Control of the Flesh or the Holy Spirit (Galatians 5:13-26)?

In the same chapter where we find the Magna Carta of Christian freedom (see Galatians 5:1), Paul also spoke strongly about walking in the Spirit and not fulfilling the lusts of the flesh. This means that as believers, we have a responsibility to discover the work of the Holy Spirit. As the Australian Anglican theologian Graeme Goldsworthy noted, "The Spirit's role is to be the powerful agent of God's saving work and to apply the word of God, the word of the gospel, to the hearts of people."[8] If life isn't in step with the Spirit, then the only other option is to live a pleasure-seeking life of self-indulgence and gratification.

In Galatians 5, Paul contrasted two phrases for believers: serve either the "desires of the flesh" or the "desires of the Spirit." He was painting a picture of two opposing ideas, and Christians must respond moment by moment to either the desires of the Holy Spirit or the desires of the flesh.[9] Which will you choose?

4. Will the Decision Have a Positive Spiritual Impact on Self (1 Corinthians 6:12; 10:23-24)?

We can ask three smaller questions to help answer this question:

- Will it build up?
- Will it profit?
- Will it help personally?[10]

Knowing this information empowers us to live Christianly. This is imperative. As Paige Patterson, president of Southwestern Baptist Seminary, noted, "The Christian, by virtue of his commitment, has accepted the responsibility of so constructing his life as to accomplish the greatest good possible."[11]

What about decisions that seem to have no spiritual impact on our life at all? We can often find insight by turning the question around: "Will this decision have a negative spiritual impact?" If something isn't good for the believer—if it doesn't build, profit, or help—it has no place, even though it might be permissible.

5. Will This Decision Addict or Enslave (1 Corinthians 6:12)?

Another way to ask this question is, Could the issue at hand lead to an activity or object having authority or power over you? One strong definition for *addiction* is that it is simply "misplaced worship," which leads to idolatry. We were created to worship, so we'll always seek to worship something. Misplaced worship is perverted intimacy or enslavement to something other than Christ. Decisions that lead to bondage aren't simply a case of mistaken freedom gone astray but a much deeper problem of perverted worship.

Some people try to address addictions in this manner: "You need to replace that bad habit with a good one." While that might sound sweet for a midday talk show, it has nothing to do with a biblical worldview. Some habits and addictions can't be replaced. Good habits don't fix bad habits any more than chocolate doughnuts win marathons.

In Exodus, we find the story of Moses and Aaron negotiating with Pharaoh for the release of Israeli slaves. No easy feat, because the slaves numbered somewhere around 2 million. When Pharaoh requested a miracle, God told Aaron to cast down his staff before the ruler and his servants. His staff became a snake. Pharaoh's magicians threw down their staffs, which also became snakes. What happened next is one of the strongest statements possible in a society that worshipped many gods. Aaron's staff-turned-snake swallowed up all of the other staffs-turned-snakes, demonstrating that there is only one true God.[12]

The freedom journey is a continual act of worship. Addiction can't be reformed, only replaced. This happens when Jesus, our one true passion, swallows up all the other desires of our lives.

6. Is the Decision Consistent with the Rule for Christian Living?

The overwhelming majority of what the Bible says about freedom focuses on the concept of service and relationships. So we can conclude that the rule for Christian living is that we filter all of our decisions through the idea of serving others. In his work *Concerning Christian Liberty*, the great reformer Martin Luther wrote,

> That all our works should be directed to the advantage of others, since every Christian has such abundance through his faith that all his other works and his whole life remain over and above wherewith to serve and benefit his neighbour of spontaneous goodwill. . . .[13]
>
> A Christian man is the most free lord of all, and subject to none; a Christian man is the most dutiful servant of all, and subject to every one.[14]

Freedom is a great source of motivation to journey through life giving ourselves to those around us. Books on leadership fill store shelves. But the truth is, *If you want to be big enough to lead, you must first be small enough to serve.*

7. Will the Decision Hurt a Fellow Believer Spiritually or Set a Spiritual Deathtrap (Romans 14:13)?

The freedom journey isn't about pleasing self but about serving others. If a decision could cause any harm to a fellow Christian spiritually, then we should avoid it. Of course, we might wonder, *Doesn't everything pose a potential threat to a weaker believer?* Sure, many activities could hypothetically become stumbling blocks or have lifelong consequences. The apostle Paul wasn't advocating a lifestyle of complete abstinence from everything. Remember that freedom focuses on how to relate and engage culture, not how to retreat to a point of isolation.

Think back to chapter 3, where we explored Paul reconciling a potential threat with an actual threat, using three scenarios involving meat sacrificed to idols (see 1 Corinthians 10:25-30). The conclusion is that if we have knowledge that an action is going to offend, then abstain for the sake of the other's conscience. In other words, we are all responsible for the knowledge we have of those inside our circles of influence. The challenge is the principle of intentional sensitivity to others.

8. Will the Decision Have a Positive Spiritual Impact on Fellow Believers (Romans 14:19; 1 Corinthians 10:23-24; Galatians 6:1-10)?

Paul wove "serving others" and "not pleasing self" throughout his letters, especially when dealing with freedom. Many discussions on freedom only pose these questions: Will something cause a negative spiritual effect on another believer? Will an action be a stumbling block or be offensive? Yet Paul took the conversation to another level. Much of his instructions have to do with a proactive approach to serving and building up one another spiritually. He urged us to "pursue the things which make for peace" (Romans 14:19, NASB). John and Paul Feinberg, two well-respected theologians, wrote, "Certain practices may be acceptable for one person, but if others saw him indulge, it might stir up strife between them. Hence, one must do what brings peace."[15]

True freedom isn't merely abstaining when we have the liberty to engage. Rather, freedom proactively seeks what could encourage a weaker Christian.

9. Does the Decision Go Against Conscience (Romans 14:14)?

Scripturally speaking, if a decision goes against the conscience of the decision maker, then the action is a sin (see Romans 14:23). On a practical note, we should exercise great patience regarding differences in conscience. Often, new followers of Christ — out of excitement for their salvation — will establish unnecessary rules to keep from falling into sin.

This can cause layers of protective fences to be set up around their lives. As a result, they might abstain altogether from certain activities. I know young believers who won't have a social-networking site because they don't want to take the chance that they might hear gossip or see something they shouldn't. As a kid, I wasn't allowed to play cards because it could lead to gambling. In any case, Paul charged believers not to go against their conscience and to accept one another as God accepts.

C. S. Lewis always seemed to instinctively communicate common ideas from an uncommon perspective, such as his thoughts on the effect of conscience on the weak and strong believer:

> We were talking about cats and dogs the other day and decided that both have consciences but the dog, being an honest, humble person, always has a bad one, but the cat is a Pharisee and always has a good one. When he sits and stares at you out of countenance, he is thanking God that he is not as these dogs, or these humans, or even as these other cats![16]

May we never become unaccepting pharisaical felines staring down our noses at other believers all the while loving our own pathetic existence.

10. Will the Decision Disrupt Fellowship and Damage Relationships Within the Community (Romans 14:15)?

Don't allow issues that are morally indifferent or secondary to damage fellowship within a community. Freedom is fueled by love and has love as its main mode of action. Without love, fellowship can't exist and only broken relationships will remain. A great principle to follow is: _Never allow opinions to be more important than relationships._ Allow love to be the motivation behind every decision. When that's the case, fellowship will stay intact and relationships will grow and mature.

11. Will the Decision Damage Reputation (Romans 14:16)?

The freedom that Christ followers have is a *good* thing (see Romans 14:16). Christ died to give us this liberty (see Galatians 5:1). Strong believers have

Prov 25:10

the responsibility to live in such a way that observers aren't tempted to speak poorly of their freedom. Paul warned against opening up opportunities for misunderstanding between the strong and weak. These conflicts could allow the outside community to speak negatively against the fellowship of believers.

Romans 14 contains a strong evangelism component. Living in light of our mission keeps focus on what's important, such as relational reputation. Reputations take time to build but just a moment to destroy. This firm word of caution challenges us with the responsibility carried by the strong in faith.

12. Will the Decision Remove Focus from the Big Picture of God's Kingdom (Romans 14:17-19)?

Many times, petty or insignificant matters rule the day. The little foxes spoil the vineyard (see Song of Solomon 2:15). How many Christians have missed the big picture of what God's kingdom is all about because they were arguing over food and drink? Many Christians beach themselves on the shores of pettiness because they chase the insignificant when all along God has purposed them for the deep waters.

Secondary issues don't make up the kingdom of God. Instead, the kingdom is focused on "righteousness and peace and joy in the Holy Spirit" (Romans 14:17). We should pursue these matters, because these qualities of the kingdom will produce unity among believers. Many of us get bogged down by reducing freedom in Christ to morally indifferent matters or secondary issues. While freedom in Christ does offer clarity, it always points back to Jesus, affording the ability to see the big picture of God's kingdom.

13. Is the Decision Being Made out of a Selfish Heart (Romans 14:20-21); Will the Decision Offend (1 Corinthians 10:32)?

Basing a decision on a sense of entitlement—and knowing it will offend—is inexcusable ungodliness. Strong believers must battle against an arrogant attitude that says, "We have special knowledge that no one else has." Remember, for even the strongest in faith among us, the best we can ever offer is refrigerator art to God.

God's perspective has a way of humbling the strong and driving out any arrogance, replacing it with an indescribable sense of gratitude. Where gratefulness exists, a self-centered heart cannot.

14. Can the Decision Be Imitated by Others Who Understand Their Freedom (1 Corinthians 10:33–11:1)?

Once it had been determined that a decision wasn't going to offend or be a stumbling block, Paul took it a step further, by asking if the decision could be imitated. This question, more than any other, leads to the most pause and deliberation. Certainly, it speaks strongly to the purposes of accountability. And much more is going on just beneath the surface. To dig deep, the decision maker must reverse his or her view and see the decision from the perspective of another in the faith. The prominent idea here is to *always seek first to understand before being understood.*

For a long time, when I read Paul's words "Imitate me, just as I also imitate Christ" (NKJV), I couldn't help but feel as though the statement was laced with pride. I'd think, *I can imitate Christ on my own, thank you very much. And by the way, Mr. Apostle-man, Jesus walked on the seashore of my life and said,* Follow me, *not,* Follow Paul as he follows me. But as I began to study the freedom we have in Christ, I was awakened to the reality that Paul wasn't calling me to follow him. Rather, he was saying that he understood his freedom and that I could imitate his freedom without fear of failure or falling. Without the baggage of pride and opinions, without worrying about pits to fall into or stumbling blocks to trip over, the journey Paul was on feels in some unexplainable way like a journey home. Together we are imitating the One who has set us free. In fact, it has become my goal to live in such a way that if someone were to imitate me, he wouldn't even know it. Instead, he would feel as though he had arrived at a place he was always intended for. In that place he would simply know it felt right—like home.

15. Is the Decision Being Made in Light of the Advancement of the Gospel of Jesus Christ (1 Corinthians 9:19-24; 10:33)?

The great reformers John Calvin and Martin Luther could not put pen to paper about freedom without speaking of the gospel. They went so far as to equate a clear understanding of liberty with a clear understanding of the gospel. When the sun sets on our journey on earth and we take our last breath on this side of eternity, what will matter? What we've done for eternity's sake is what counts. Did I love God exhaustively? Love my family because of that love for God? Seek to have influence on others that would last for eternity?

The longer we live, shorter and shorter grows the list of things in life that truly matter. David Livingstone, the great missionary to Africa, said it this way after burying his wife: "I shall place no value on anything I possess, or on anything I may do, except in relation to the kingdom of Christ."[17]

The apostle Paul expressed his desire to live out his freedom in light of advancing the gospel. In 1 Corinthians 9:19-23, he wrote:

> Even though I am free of the demands and expectations of everyone, I have voluntarily become a servant to any and all in order to reach a wide range of people: religious, nonreligious, meticulous moralists, loose-living immoralists, the defeated, the demoralized—whoever. I didn't take on their way of life. I kept my bearings in Christ—but I entered their world and tried to experience things from their point of view. I've become just about every sort of servant there is in my attempts to lead those I meet into a God-saved life. I did all this because of the Message. I didn't just want to talk about it; I wanted to be *in* on it! (MSG)

16. Will the Decision Glorify God (1 Corinthians 10:31); Will the Decision Make a Big Deal About Jesus (Galatians 6:11-16)?

This is the ultimate question in the "how to believe" grid. Shouldn't the goal of every Christian be to make the redemptive work of Christ central to life and to glorify God for all that he is and all that he does? As the old tradition says, "This is the chief end of man, to glorify God and enjoy him forever."

What does it mean to glorify God? John Piper, pastor of Bethlehem Baptist Church in Minneapolis, Minnesota, and author of more than thirty books, provided this answer: "If God made us for His glory, it is clear that we should live for His glory. Our duty comes from God's design. . . . It does not mean to make Him glorious. It means to acknowledge His glory, to value it above all things, and to make it known."[18] It sounds simple. And it might even come across as preachy. But in the end, the goal is Christ.

CONCLUSION

We live in a world of smoke and mirrors. We almost expect to be tricked and confused because nothing is as it seems. Ambiguity has become an expected part of life in our culture. But the purpose in understanding our freedom is to dispel in the smoke and mirrors, letting in the light to shine clarity on some of the more complicated and confusing issues we face.

The next five chapters will do just that. We will discern how to develop godly beliefs on the following issues:

The world is confussion by its lies. God's light of the world, Jesus, clarifies + is compeling us closer to Him.

- Homosexuality
- The Cyber World
- Social Drinking
- Entertainment
- Humanitarian Efforts

I've chosen to explore these areas using the sixteen "how to believe" questions because these topics represent secondary issues of our Christian faith that vary widely in shades of gray. Some seem almost black and white, while others might seem barely worth exploring through this grid. The point isn't to tell you what I believe about these elephants in the room, or even what you should believe. Rather, I hope to demonstrate how I came to my own conclusions so that you can then do the same with hundreds of other issues. You might not agree with where I land on these areas, but I trust the process will prove itself invaluable.

So grab a cup of over-priced coffee and let's start chasing elephants!

CHAPTER 6

ELEPHANT 1: HOMOSEXUALITY

A young man named Ethan sits in a church pew every Sunday surrounded by family, friends, and strangers. Although the room is crowded, he has never felt more alone.

Loneliness is only part of Ethan's increasing confusion, and the fear of condemnation haunts every part of his being both day and night. He sings the songs, but they are only words. He listens to the sermon, but it is only words. He is surrounded by conversation and laughter from happy relationships swirling around him, but again they are only words. Ethan is drowning in a sea of white noise with no sign of relief in sight. He wonders if relief even exists for people like him. People like him? *Why has God created me?* he often ponders in the midst of his ambiguous existence. Resistance to what is unnatural but at the same time seems right in some way is only a temporary solution. His breath now becomes short, and he walks around with the feeling of a heavy weight on his chest.

Ethan soon departed from his white-noise existence and graduated from high school. A new chapter of life began, accompanied by a new search for meaning and identity. Full of wonder and fear, he stepped foot onto a university campus. His former life seemed light-years away; in his new world, honest questions were asked and straightforward answers were provided or at least discussed. Before long, Ethan was fully immersed in his new world, and in an even shorter time, he became intoxicated with the freedom that accompanied it. Here, he encountered people asking many of the same questions and sharing many of the same feelings.

A period of same-sex experimentation followed, and time and truth soon became irrelevant for Ethan. All that mattered was that the desires of his inner being were fed. But soon, his desires transformed into a monster that at best was all consuming and at worst a constant reminder of his fragile mortality. Ethan's confidence in this new world and all that it offered was slowly challenged by the lack of clarity and fulfillment he was hoping it would provide. Again, time didn't matter, and truth was only a myth that seemed to bounce off the walls like the screams of a little kid yelling in a big room. As he entered the next season, his life, on the surface, appeared to be normal. But underneath was pain and bitterness.

The journey continued on for years and seemed to pass by both slowly and quickly at the same time. Slowly, because the loneliness and periodic silence seemed to permeate every cell of his body. Quickly, because the monster inside raged on. As the latter stages of adulthood and life approached in a steady and unconscious manner, so did the evolution of this thought. Ethan went to work running the marketing division for a shoe company surrounded by the busyness of his job. People completed their assigned tasks, conversed at the watercooler, made fun of the boss, and went out for a beer after work. Yet it was all nothing more than empty chatter to him.

Outside of work, Ethan continued on with his ever-changing community of people who had the same inclinations he did, yet he felt completely alone. The loneliness reminded him of another time in his life when he was much younger and had not yet become engrossed in his current lifestyle. He was again the young man sitting in the pew wondering if there was any way out of this white-noise existence.

As many of us read Ethan's story, our hearts are burdened for him. We might ask, "Does he ever find Jesus and a community of believers that can extend the grace and love of God to him?"

What if I told you that there are thousands of Ethans sitting in thousands of pews every week? The issue of homosexuality isn't a distant story. Rather, it's a reality unfolding right before our eyes. Consider this: Could someone stand in your community of believers—whether a local church or small group—and confess to homosexual inclinations without the risk of what can only be described as an unspoken excommunication? Does such an inclination automatically mean, "You can be in the church, just not part of the family?"

I'm not writing this out of some righteous indignation I have toward people in the church, but out of a deep sense of conviction I have upon reflection of my own journey. You see, I've been guilty of the "limp wrist" jokes and of replacing an honest look at the Scriptures with quick and easy slogans I've heard some preacher say.

In fact, my slogans and bumper-sticker theology are wrong. And because they are wrong, I have misrepresented Christ and misunderstood what it means to be salt and light.

One of the great tasks the church faces today is how to respond with a Christlike love to those struggling with a homosexual lifestyle. Understand that the love of God is a magnet. Everyone wants it. Everyone was created to experience it. And when that type of love is the central motivation to ministry and life, a diverse group of sinners will cross our path. But as we choose who we will demonstrate Christ's love to, we display the worst kind of arrogance. Do we really think we can segregate the love of God?

I believe that to even ask the question of whether or not our church will extend grace and forgiveness is a strike against us. Forgiveness is something we must live. It's more than a choice; it's a calling and command. Because we have been forgiven, extending forgiveness is the natural response to grace.

Without a doubt, one of the single greatest issues, or elephants, facing the church is homosexuality. As I write these words, one of today's headlines in *The New York Times* is "Lutheran Group Eases Limits on Gay Clergy." The article begins, "After an emotional debate over the authority of Scripture and the limits of biblical inclusiveness, leaders of the country's largest Lutheran denomination voted Friday to allow gay men and lesbians in committed relationships to serve as members of the clergy."[1]

The article goes on to point out that this is not the first mainline denomination to allow gay clergy, just the latest. This is an elephant that must be approached with biblically informed thought and attitude — in other words, with grace and truth. To know what the Bible says yet not act as the Bible teaches is not acceptable. If you don't have a good balance, you won't properly represent Jesus in our culture. Therefore, we will approach this subject through the "how to believe" grid we formulated in the previous chapter. But first we need to give a definition of homosexuality.

WHAT IS HOMOSEXUALITY? CAN ONE BE BORN GAY?

These might seem like ridiculous questions at first. But answer this: Is homosexuality something you are, something you do, or both? In other words, is someone born genetically predisposed to a homosexual lifestyle, having no choice in the matter? Or is the homosexual lifestyle completely a personal choice?

For much of my life, I never questioned why someone would engage in homosexual activity. In fact, the extent of my argument was that the Bible condemns those actions and the homosexual chooses to be the way he or she is. But what if the desire to engage in homosexual activity can't be helped? What if someone is simply attracted to others of the same sex and doesn't know how or why this attraction exists? I ask these questions because of my own inclination to be very heavy handed in truth but not grace.

The source of homosexuality is yet to be scientifically or clinically discovered. Since the genetic or psychological causes of such an orientation might or might not ever be understood, we won't take time to examine various studies that at the end of the day raise more questions than provide answers. Instead, we'll examine key biblical texts that address homosexuality. Let's take an honest look at this issue and then wrestle with how the body of Christ can extend grace and forgiveness.

Before beginning, a mega-idea needs to be understood: *The Bible does not condemn homosexual inclination or orientation; rather, the Scriptures clearly condemn homosexual activity or behavior.* That doesn't mean that all sexual orientations have the same moral equivalence. It simply points out the fact that orientations don't necessarily determine identity.

To start, we need a clear definition of *homosexuality*.

Andrew Sullivan, a leading figure in the homosexual community, defined the term to mean "someone who is constitutively, emotionally and sexually, attracted to the same sex."[2] William Lane Craig, a respected and accomplished defender of the faith, shared a similar definition: "Being homosexual is a state or an orientation; a person who has a homosexual orientation might not ever express that orientation in actions."[3] Others would define *homosexuality* differently, as having multiple same-sex encounters.[4] Notice that the first two definitions focus on attraction and inclination while the third focuses on activity. This then begs the question, is homosexuality being or doing?

A clear understanding of the New Testament leads to the conclusion that if Jesus or Paul had been asked this question, they would have shaken their heads in disgust and made some statement about how we don't get it. The gospel of grace means that when we make a declaration to follow Christ, our identity is transformed on all levels and we are saved to good works. The follower of God doesn't find his or her identity in sexual orientation, but rather in Christ. In other words, a supernatural effect takes place on both who one is and what one does. With this *being* and *doing* identity in mind, for the purposes of our discussion, we'll define *homosexuality* as "both the desire to and engagement in homosexual behavior." Examine carefully the following scriptures — Mark 12:28-31; John 15:8; 2 Corinthians 5:17-21; James 2:14-20 — and you'll see in this idea of being and doing, that identity and action are intrinsically bound to each other. Or to put it more bluntly, who I am and what I do cannot be separated.

HOW TO BELIEVE: HOMOSEXUALITY

What Does the Explicit Moral Will of God Say Concerning Homosexuality?

You might remember that the first step to understanding freedom in Christ is to ask if the particular issue is directly addressed in the Scriptures. In this case, six biblical texts deal explicitly with homosexuality. We'll discover that homosexuality is defined as a sin in the Bible. We must first note that no one sin is more respectable than others; all sin breaks the heart of God and should therefore break the hearts of his followers. Having said that, while all sin breaks the heart of God, not all sin bears the same consequence. Most would agree that a complexity of issues is involved with homosexuality and the potential physical consequences that follow. But for the purposes of this chapter, we'll keep our conversation within the context of what Scripture teaches. The first of the six passages is found in Genesis 19.

Genesis 19:1-13

At this point in redemptive history, Abraham was becoming more and more prominent while Lot, who resided in Sodom, was nearing his exit from the pages of Scripture. The city of Sodom had become so evil that it was enslaved to its own fleshly desires. God had informed Abraham of his plans to destroy the city, and in one of the most compassionate intercessory prayers in all of Scripture, Abraham begged for the lives of the citizens of Sodom (see Genesis 18:22-33). Abraham asked God to spare the city if fifty righteous individuals could be found. God agreed, and Abraham continued his conversation with a series of "what ifs": What if there were forty-five righteous? What if there were only forty or thirty or twenty or just ten? In the end, the void of righteousness was so vast and so deep that God determined judgment by destroying the city.

In Genesis 19, two angels entered the city of Sodom and met Lot at the city gates. Lot persuaded them to come to his house to enjoy refreshment and a night of rest before they carried on with their journey. Reluctantly, they agreed. But then the story took a dark and dangerous turn: "Before they lay down, the men of the city, the men of Sodom, both young and old, all the people to the last man, surrounded the house" (verse 4). Remember, Abraham had just pleaded for an all-out search for just a handful of righteous individuals. Yet now all of the men of the city had surrounded Lot's house. While there is much that is not articulated in this text, the writer did point out that "young and old" had surrounded the house. John Calvin noted,

It shows how completely destitute they were of all remaining shame; for, neither did any gravity restrain the old, nor any modesty, suitable to their age, restrain the young . . . all regard for honor is gone, and that the order of nature was perverted, when he says, that young and old flew together from the extreme parts of the city.[5]

Then the account speaks explicitly to the issue of homosexuality: "And they called to Lot, 'Where are the men who came to you tonight? Bring them out to us, that we may know them'" (verse 5). The key part of this verse that we'll examine further is the final phrase "that we may know them." Understanding this text depends on our interpretation of the verb "to know." The Hebrew root "to know" appears a total of 944 times in a variety of forms and expresses a multitude of shades of knowledge gained by the senses.[6]

There are two specific reasons we can conclude that the men of Sodom wanted to have homosexual relations with Lot's guests. First, "to know" is used throughout the Old Testament for sexual intercourse on the part of both men and women (see Genesis 4:1; 19:8; Numbers 31:17,35; Judges 11:39; 1 Samuel 1:19; 1 Kings 1:4). The most prominent is Genesis 4:1, which reads, "Adam knew Eve his wife, and she conceived and bore Cain." "To know" is also used to describe sexual perversions such as sodomy and rape (see Judges 19:22,25). So, while a wide variety of uses exists for the verb "to know," it is certainly consistent with other texts that in this circumstance it means "to know sexually."

The second reason we can assume the men of Sodom intended to have homosexual relations with these angels is offered by a strong statement in Jude 1:7: "Sodom and Gomorrah and the surrounding cities, which likewise indulged in sexual immorality and pursued unnatural desire, serve as an example by undergoing a punishment of eternal fire." The people of Sodom "pursued unnatural desire," or as this has also been translated, "strange flesh." This phrase encompasses different kinds of sexual perversions but unquestionably includes homosexual activity.

We all know the end of the story—the incineration of the entire city, along with Gomorrah — probably much better than the events leading up to it. Abraham's intercessory prayer demonstrates the role of godly people within a culture, who should be all about compassion. In fact, we need to stress God's willingness to listen and his patience to judge — as if judgment were the last option. Knowing only the end of any particular Bible story is probably something many of us are guilty of, but it's a problem. Without knowing the full story, many times we miss how it applies to understanding our role in culture.

Did God destroy Sodom and Gomorrah because of the existence of homosexuality within the culture? Jude 1:7 certainly paints that picture. God destroyed Sodom because "the outcry . . . is great and their sin is very grave" (Genesis 18:20). The phrase "the outcry" might seem confusing at first glance. But consider this: Could it be that our very sin screams defilement against all of heaven and God himself? Remember Genesis 4:10, "And the LORD said, 'What have you done? The voice of your brother's blood is crying to me from the ground.'" Sin has a voice, but many times only one listener. Sin also has a message, and there is only one proper response. In fact, it's an interesting thought experiment to consider that the sin we commit in private might in reality have the most public audience.

The voice of sin is loud, and the message of sin is injustice and corruption. God alone can hear this appeal and respond. He heard the outcry of Sodom and saw that evil didn't just exist randomly. The entire city had chosen to join hands and slide down sin's slippery slope into a cesspool of depravity and immorality. I hope that we'll never be able to imagine the depths these people had fallen to, although we're capable of doing more than just imagining. God didn't destroy Sodom just because of the existence of homosexual behavior. He destroyed the city because homosexuality dominated and was celebrated, pointing to a picture of complete immorality that had infiltrated the entire city.

I know these conclusions can be a tough pill to swallow for some of us who have friends who consider themselves homosexuals. But this passage and the texts that we'll examine next are clear. Also keep in mind that at this point we're only looking at what the Bible says and trying to gain an understanding of God's attitude toward homosexuality. At the end of the chapter, we'll examine what our response should be.

Leviticus 18:22; 20:13

For many of us, Leviticus might be a book we've never read. Or if we have read it, we approached it with the idea that it has no relevance to modern Christianity. In reality, Leviticus is a book that not only has relevance, it also answers a timeless question: What is the acceptable way to live before a holy God?

It's always essential to understand verses in the context of which they were written. The two statements we're going to examine are part of answering life's timeless question. We don't need to run from them, but we do need to understand them if we want to know how to live and approach God. Some advocates for homosexuality say that these prohibitions are no longer relevant today because they are found in the Old Testament. However, the problem with this argument is that the New Testament reaffirms the authority and relevance of Old Testament prohibitions against homosexual behavior. This demonstrates to us that these prohibitions were not simply part of a ceremonial law but part of God's everlasting moral law.[7]

> You shall not lie with a male as with a woman; it is an abomination. (Leviticus 18:22)

> If a man lies with a male as with a woman, both of them have committed an abomination; they shall surely be put to death; their blood is upon them. (Leviticus 20:13)

No doubt, these verses contain strong words. Both provide a short but explicit description of homosexual activity and then call it "an abomination." The term *abomination* refers to an act that is abhorrent or repugnant. The NIV translates this word to read "detestable." Four Hebrew words are translated into the English "abomination." Of those four, the one used in these verses is used most frequently. It indicates a violation of an established custom or ritual that, in turn, brings the judgment of God.[8] Simply put, an abomination is something that dishonors God's holiness. It occurs when you choose to do something contrary to both the law of God and the order of nature. These verses also indicate that whatever role someone plays in homosexual behavior, aggressor or passive, both have committed an abomination.

As I write these words, my heart is heavy. I need to pause and declare that having a biblical worldview isn't always easy and the vast majority of the time has a very countercultural feel. To those who would say a strong "Amen! Detestable!" to the above truths concerning homosexuality, I'm afraid you're already missing the point. Truth need not always be communicated through a megaphone on the mountaintop, but sometimes through tears in the valley. If pride, not compassion, characterizes your attitude over this sin, even though you may be a child of God, you certainly have an unchristian attitude. Let's carry on.

Before we examine New Testament texts, there is that little issue about "they shall surely be put to death; their blood is upon them." Is homosexuality a crime punishable by death? What relevance does such a statement have on current culture?

First, we must understand that in the Old Testament, the purpose of "God's law was to restrain sin, not to reform sinners; the penalties He imposed were for the purpose of upholding His law, not improving the offenders."[9] Second, although included on an extensive list of capital crimes that were punishable by death in that day, homosexuality wouldn't be subjected to the same punishment today. This list includes striking or cursing a parent (see Exodus 21:15,17), breaking the Sabbath (see Exodus 31:14), blaspheming God (see Leviticus 24:10-16), engaging in occult practices (see Exodus 22:18), prophesying falsely (see Deuteronomy 13:1-5), adultery (see Leviticus 20:10), rape (see Deuteronomy 22:25), sex before marriage (see Deuteronomy 22:13-30), incest (see Leviticus 20:11-12), bestiality (see Leviticus 20:15-16), kidnapping (see Exodus 21:16), idolatry (see Exodus 34:14), false witness in a case involving a capital crime (see Deuteronomy 19:16-21), and killing a human intentionally (see Exodus 21:12). Interestingly, all of these offenses have to do with the family unit. As a society, Israel was founded on a covenant with God. So offenses that threatened this covenant relationship were the same as crimes p̶nishable in the name of the highest authority in the state.[10] God was abo͟ _____ he'd promised them. Preserv͟ ͟ ͟he nation. These offenses ͟ ͟e of Israel would underst͟ ͟elationship with God. I͟ ͟ger served as the basis f͟ ͟sted, with a hier-archal ͟ ͟ture of crime and the ra͟ ͟rael's legislation.[11] Let m͟ ͟e guilty of a moral offens͟

U͟ ͟Testament forbids hom͟ ͟omination punish-able ͟ ͟ a city addicted to this ͟

Handwritten note on overlay: TASMAR tolcapone 100mg/200mg tablets — Matt 19:29 — Luke 14:26 — Ps 16:8 — Roche

Does the New Testament forbid homosexua͟ ͟avior? If so, is it with the same intensity? The first text we'll examine demonstrates the relevancy and realistic nature of Scripture.

1 Corinthians 6:9-10

The apostle Paul wrote to the church in Corinth,

> Do you not know that the <u>unrighteous</u> *(unsaved)* will not inherit the kingdom of God? Do not be deceived: neither the sexually immoral, nor idolaters, nor adulterers, nor men <u>who practice</u> homosexuality, nor thieves, nor the greedy, nor drunkards, nor revilers, nor swindlers will inherit the kingdom of God. (1 Corinthians 6:9-10)

The first statement we'll examine is "the unrighteous will not inherit the kingdom of God." The term *unrighteous* speaks of unrighteous people in general, not believers who are in danger of losing their salvation if they committed any of the sins in the catalog that follows. *Unrighteousness* refers to those who continually do wrong or who live as if God's moral standards don't exist. Therefore, the list of sins in these verses is not describing people who are Christians and will lose their salvation by committing these sins. Rather, the list describes those who are not followers of God. In other words, people who aren't Christians — and, therefore, who are unrighteous people) — will not go to heaven when they die. Make no mistake about it: This is what unrighteousness looks like. *The Message* words it this way: "Unjust people who don't care about God will not be joining in his kingdom."

Next, let's examine possibly the most explicit statement in Scripture dealing with this issue. Paul wrote that those who do not care about God or his moral will are not going to be part of his kingdom. The apostle then gave a catalog that includes the sexually immoral, idolaters, adulterers, men who practice homosexuality, thieves, greedy, drunkards, revilers, and swindlers. While this isn't an exhaustive list, it did survey the landscape of lifestyles typically found outside of the Christian community in Corinth.

For our purposes, we'll zero in on the phrase "men who practice homosexuality." The Greek words being used to describe homosexual behavior are speaking of the passive partner in homosexual sex, which could also include male prostitution, as well as the one who takes the active male role in homosexual sex. I warned you this was an explicit passage! Therefore, Paul was teaching that whatever the role — whether passive, active, or passive by selling off your body for unnatural sex — this lifestyle does not describe those who will go to heaven.

A natural question to ask here is, "What about those who claim to be Christian and homosexual at the same time?" At this point, the Bible is very clear: Someone who chooses to adhere to a homosexual lifestyle — or to any of the other lifestyles mentioned, including alcoholism or thievery — and is unrepentant about that lifestyle shall not be in heaven. Paul wasn't referring to those who struggle, repent, and continue to struggle. Rather, he was writing about those who never repent, which is why he called them the unrighteous. The reason this question is relevant has to do with the casual perspective some people have about salvation. If your view of salvation is to pray a little prayer and then add "becoming a Christ follower" to your résumé of life experiences, there would certainly be room for a homosexual lifestyle along with many other things.

However, following Christ is not one of many experiences. Instead, it is the defining experience that serves as a gateway to a new identity. Think of it this way: The decision to turn from sin and place your faith in Christ determines all your other decisions, including ones that have to do with sexual behavior. There is nothing casual about deciding to surrender your life to follow Jesus. Christ himself said in Luke 14:33 that "any one of you who does not renounce all that he has cannot be my disciple." As *The Message* says, "Simply put, if you're not willing to take what is dearest to you, whether plans or people, and kiss it good-bye, you can't be my disciple."

Part of following Jesus is counting the cost. What does it cost us to follow him? The answer: everything that has to do with us. And what do we get in return? Everything we could ever need in Jesus.

1 Timothy 1:8-11

The apostle Paul also addressed the subject of homosexuality in a letter to his young student, Timothy, who was serving as the pastor of the church in Ephesus.

> Now we know that the law is good, if one uses it lawfully, understanding this, that the law is not laid down for the just but for the lawless and disobedient, for the ungodly and sinners, for the unholy and profane, for those who strike their fathers and mothers, for murderers, the sexually immoral, men who practice homosexuality, enslavers, liars, perjurers, and whatever else is contrary to sound doctrine, in accordance with the glorious gospel of the blessed God with which I have been entrusted. (1 Timothy 1:8-11)

In many ways, this passage echoes 1 Corinthians 6:9-10, while at the same time elaborating on the purpose of the law. Judaism divided the Old Testament scriptures (which were the only scriptures available) into three sections: the Law, the Prophets, and the Writings. The Law refers to the writings of Moses, also called the Pentateuch, which are the first five books of the Bible. This was understood to be the explicit moral will of God. Again, Paul provided a catalog of sins in 1 Timothy 1:8-11, and the law applies to people who commit these sins. Interestingly, the sins mentioned parallel five of the Ten Commandments in Exodus 20:

COMMANDMENT NUMBER	COMMANDMENT	SIN
Number 5	Honor your father and your mother.	"those who strike their fathers and mothers"
Number 6	You shall not murder.	"for murderers"
Number 7	You shall not commit adultery.	"the sexually immoral, men who practice homosexuality"
Number 8	You shall not steal.	"enslavers"
Number 9	You shall not bear false witness against your neighbor.	"liars, perjurers"

What we discover here is that Paul forbade homosexual behavior, and he directly connected this command with God's foundational law about how human beings are to interact with each other. The first five commandments speak to our relationship with God and the second five speak to our relationship with others. Therefore, the New Testament confirms, develops, and builds on what the Old Testament teaches. In addition, this passage helps us further interpret, among other things, the seventh commandment. "You shall not commit adultery" speaks to more than just one spouse cheating on another. It speaks to anything outside of God's intended purpose for sex. In other words, it refers to any sexual sin, which includes lust, unclean thoughts, fooling around, rape, incest, and, yes, homosexuality.

Romans 1:18-32

Now we'll turn our attention to the most extensive and important writings on homosexual activity in the New Testament. This is also the only place in Scripture that explicitly mentions lesbianism.

> For the wrath of God is revealed from heaven against all ungodliness and unrighteousness of men, who by their unrighteousness suppress the truth. For what can be known about God is plain to them, because God has shown it to them. For his invisible attributes, namely, his eternal power and divine nature, have been clearly perceived, ever since the creation of the world, in the things that have been made. So they are without excuse. For although they knew God, they did not honor him as God or give thanks to him, but they became futile in their thinking, and their foolish hearts were darkened. Claiming to be wise, they became fools, and exchanged the glory of the immortal God for images resembling mortal man and birds and animals and reptiles.
>
> Therefore God gave them up in the lusts of their hearts to impurity, to the dishonoring of their bodies among themselves, because they exchanged the truth about God for a lie and worshiped and served the creature rather than the Creator, who is blessed forever! Amen.
>
> For this reason God gave them up to dishonorable passions. For their women exchanged natural relations for

those that are contrary to nature; and the men likewise gave up natural relations with women and were consumed with passion for one another, men committing shameless acts with men and receiving in themselves the due penalty for their error.

And since they did not see fit to acknowledge God, God gave them up to a debased mind to do what ought not to be done. They were filled with all manner of unrighteousness, evil, covetousness, malice. They are full of envy, murder, strife, deceit, maliciousness. They are gossips, slanderers, haters of God, insolent, haughty, boastful, inventors of evil, disobedient to parents, foolish, faithless, heartless, ruthless. Though they know God's decree that those who practice such things deserve to die, they not only do them but give approval to those who practice them. (Romans 1:18-32)

The strength of this passage is that it demonstrates the downward spiral a society takes toward the acceptance and celebration of homosexuality. We'll chart the journey for which the destination is "no return." By that, I certainly don't mean that the love of God cannot reach into the depths of a dark and morally decaying society and rescue lost sinners. I simply mean that there seems to be a point from which very few look up and ask him to. These are the steps that can be outlined from this text:

Step One: The unrighteous become oblivious to the obvious truth (verses 18-21).
Step Two: Man falls in love with his own vanity (verse 21).
Step Three: The heart that is empty is full of darkness (verse 21).
Step Four: A new wisdom is claimed (verse 22).
Step Five: God's truth is exchanged for a lie (verse 25).
Step Six: They worship creation, including their own bodies (verses 23-25).
Step Seven: God gives them over to their sinful desires (verse 26).
Step Eight: They engage in homosexual activity (verses 26-27).

Step Nine: They receive just penalties and consequences for their
actions (verse 27).

Step Ten: Homosexuality is approved and celebrated in culture
(verse 32).

EXTENDING GRACE AND FORGIVENESS

In the final part of this chapter, it's important to focus on how our freedom in Christ enables us to extend grace and forgiveness. This is something the church hasn't done a very good job of. Even though with this
issue we only asked the first question from the "how to believe" grid, that
doesn't make some of the other evidences of freedom obsolete. Our freedom should motivate us to serve others — even those living in direct contradiction to God's moral laws — so that they too might become followers
of Christ. Freedom should also motivate us toward a Christlike attitude
and the building up of community. Therefore, if we properly understand
our freedom as believers when we approach the issue of homosexuality,
then the following will be the outworking of our freedom as we seek to be
ambassadors for Christ.

Understand Your Role: To Be Abraham, Not God

It's easy to read Genesis 19 and say, "Well, they got what they deserved."
It's easy, but it's not right. What if a very prominent homosexual that
you're familiar with — whether in Hollywood, sports, politics, or wherever — were to be diagnosed with a terminal type of cancer? In that first
moment when you hear the news, if you were to be completely honest,
what would be your attitude toward that individual and his condition?
Would you somehow feel more proud about being a Christian because
someone who isn't is now dying? Or would your attitude possibly be, "If
you play with fire, you're going to get burned"? Or maybe your response
could be one of silent vindication and self-righteousness? If that's the case,
then we don't have the faintest idea of what grace and forgiveness are.
You see, above all else, the following should be evident: Because we have
escaped judgment only by the grace of God, we should therefore desire

that no one experience the fate we all deserved. Judgment is reserved for God.

So let's stop trying to wear the God hat. It doesn't fit our human heads anyway. Instead, let's start serving. Being Abraham might not always yield the results you want, but it is a hat that certainly fits.

Communicate the Truth About Sin with a Broken Heart

As we've already admitted, the biblical truth about homosexuality can be a tough pill to swallow, especially in a culture that increasingly celebrates the idea. In fact, as David Kinnaman, researcher and president of The Barna Group, has found, many people outside the Christian faith and even young churchgoers have an increasing lack of concern about homosexuality.[13] However, we must communicate the truth about sin, but only after our hearts first break for sinners. Sin fractures every human soul. In our conversations, we must never be guilty of positioning one sin as more "sinful" than another.

Remember, we're not given a right standing before God because we are heterosexual versus homosexual. You don't go to heaven because you fall in love with someone of the opposite sex. All that will matter when we step into eternity is Jesus. For our purposes, we've stayed within the bounds of what the Bible says about the issue and how our freedom should shape our attitude. Still, this elephant will not go away, and we need to approach this issue with grace and truth.

Avoid Bumper-Sticker Theology

Have you ever heard some Christian deliver his entire argument against homosexuality using only bumper-sticker phrases such as "God didn't create Adam and Steve; he created Adam and Eve!"? This statement and approach is incorrect for two reasons.

First, the argument is incomplete; this is where cute-sounding slogans fail over and over again. Like an air gun, they make a lot of noise but there are no bullets, so they're ineffective. To offer a complete biblical argument is to present a thorough treatment of the issue, which I've tried to do here. The goal has been to survey the biblical landscape and then to focus in on particular texts with an effort to both gain the big picture and understand the essentials concerning homosexuality. It's important to remember that an incomplete argument is more likely to represent Satan; we only need to remember the fall of man to find evidence of this.

Second, the bumper-sticker argument is incorrect because it doesn't represent the attitude of Christ. In my experience, the person who doesn't possess a Christlike attitude toward homosexuality is usually someone who will either laugh at a joke about homosexuals or make jokes himself. However, depravity and unrighteousness are never laughing matters; in fact, they represent a sin for which many Christians need to repent.

As Christ followers, the reality we face is that there probably are people all around us who are bound in a lifestyle of homosexuality. Our attitude toward their sin could in fact determine the amount of influence we're able to have in this life and the one to come. *I find less + less humor on TV yet I have more joy from the filling of the Spirit.*

Love the Sinner, Hate Your Own Sin

All my life I've been taught this statement: "Love the sinner and hate the sin." Unfortunately, this statement doesn't mean what it used to because it has become another bumper-sticker slogan that oversimplifies very complex sexual issues and baggage. Those living a homosexual lifestyle find much of their identity rooted in their sexuality. So when the words "God loves the sinner and hates the sin" are said, many times that is interpreted "because God hates my sin, he and his followers also hate me as a person." In his book *unChristian*, David Kinnaman offered groundbreaking research supporting the existence of this perception. He summarized it this way:

> The gay issue has become the "big one," the negative image most likely to be intertwined with Christianity's reputation. It is also the dimension that most clearly demonstrates the unChristian faith to young people today, surfacing a spate of negative perceptions: judgmental, bigoted, sheltered, right-wingers, hypocritical, insincere, and uncaring. Outsiders [meaning non-Christians] say our hostility toward gays—not

just opposition to homosexual politics and behaviors but dis-
dain for gay individuals—has become virtually synonymous
with the Christian faith.[14]

Kinnaman went on to articulate that more than 90 percent of those
interviewed outside the Christian faith said "antihomosexual" accurately
describes present-day Christianity.[15] This is the perception. It's our fault,
and we must change it.

How can that happen? Well, I can tell you that complicated issues are
rarely solved overnight. It will take time. But with the freedom we have
in Christ as the motivation and guide, our churches can become places
of grace and forgiveness. Maybe the best way to start is by looking in the
mirror to remind ourselves that the love of Jesus rescued this sinner from
hell. Jesus died for and because of my sin. And I have enough sin in my
own life to worry about.

Maybe the best place to start is by loving the sinner and hating my
own sin.

ELEPHANT 2:
THE CYBER WORLD

Every morning when twenty-two-year-old Kate wakes up, she rolls over and looks at her smart phone to see if anyone has sent her a text message or e-mail. After responding to a few messages, she taps an icon on the screen that immediately takes her to a networking site where she updates her status and gets updated on everyone else's. While there, she buys weapons from a friend who is playing the same online game about organized crime that she is. Kate then scrolls over to a less violent game that involves harvesting crops, which she'll sell to expand her virtual agricultural endeavors. Finally, Kate sends out a short message through another social-networking medium announcing to all her friends that she is in fact awake and feeling happy. And this is all before she even gets out of bed!

Most of us use the Internet virtually every day to communicate, work, and play. It's a network of networks that is host to information for millions of organizations from governments to nonprofits. I refer to it as the "cyber world" because of how vast and great it is. In fact, most of us would have a hard time imagining our lives without it. Think about how it affects our communication and media consumption. Without the Internet, what good would our cell phones be? I guess we would have to use them for talking again. How would we update our friends on our latest comings and goings or watch a waterskiing squirrel? While the Internet was actually conceived in the late 1950s and early 1960s, it wasn't until the early 1990s that its popularity began to soar.

In less than twenty years, the number of people who use the cyber world has skyrocketed. Consider the following: In Africa, more than 67 million people, or 6.8 percent of the population, use the Internet; in Asia, more than 738 million, or 19.4 percent of the population; in Europe, more than 418 million, or 52 percent of the population; and here in North America, almost 253 million, or 74.2 percent of the population. In all, a quarter of the world's population uses the Internet.[1] And in the United States, at least three out of every four individuals use the Internet.

Clearly, the online world occupies a predominant chunk of our attention and time, and we need to approach it with a spirit of intentionality fueled by a biblical worldview. While some would argue that technology is neutral, no one would claim that the actions taking place inside the medium are neutral. Every decision we make comes out of our worldview. So any and all decisions are influenced by that worldview. In short, we can't separate our worldview from how we operate within the world. As Cedarville University president Bill Brown has said on many occasions, "You may not live what you profess but you will live what you believe . . . it is inescapable."

For our purposes, we'll focus on one of the more prominent ways that sixteen- to twenty-nine-year-olds use the Internet: social networking. In the previous chapter we only utilized one question from the "how to believe" grid, but in this chapter we'll call on several questions to help us become convinced in our own minds. You can choose to utilize more or different questions from the grid to help you. But as I network, communicate, and keep in touch with family, friends, students, and ministry leaders, these are the questions that have helped me the most.

HOW TO BELIEVE: SOCIAL NETWORKING

Am I Representing the Attitude of Christ in My Social Networking (Romans 15:1-13)?

We've looked at a number of Scripture passages on freedom that remind us the attitude of Christ is demonstrated in service, community, and worship. Because attitude is a great indicator of motive, one of the best ways to answer this question is to start by asking, "What's my purpose for social networking?"

Social networking is made up of online communities of people with shared interests. This virtual network affords individuals the ability to stay connected and informed through text and video. This is a great tool that has opened up a world of communication opportunities. But as we communicate through this medium, we should do so in a way that represents Jesus.

As with all aspects of life, Scripture calls us to engage in any activity while thinking and acting Christianly. This means that if you're a football player, then someone should be able to observe what Jesus would look like in shoulder pads. If you're a full-time student, then others should be able to see what Jesus would look like attending a university. If you work at a restaurant, then others should be able to witness what Jesus would look like waiting tables. In the same way Jesus becomes our identity in every area of life, He must also reign in our social networking.

Unfortunately, for some people, the cyber world, and all that it offers, represents a different reality. Because of its relative anonymity, the online world is a place where the rules are different. If you find yourself going to the Internet to escape your true reality, then you must ask yourself if that's a Christlike attitude. If we're not careful, we can fall into a trap where the Internet becomes an unrealistic reality for us.

Reality must always be defined through the lens of what the Bible teaches. The challenge is to filter our activity in the cyber world through a biblical worldview and fix our eyes on Jesus. If we're focused on Christ, then we will represent him well, even on social-networking sites. It might sound a bit corny, but always be answering the question, "How would Jesus navigate the cyber world?"

Are My Social Networking Activities Under the Control of the Flesh or the Holy Spirit (Galatians 5:13-26)?

As we've already discovered, the flesh and the Holy Spirit are at war against each other. The flesh wants to pursue sinful self-interests, and the Spirit wants that which pleases God.

A former employer of mine used to tell me, "Any of us are only one step away from stupid at any time." I think the same idea applies in the cyber world; at any moment we are just one click away from sin. Satan is always looking for a place to get a foothold in our lives and that includes our online networks. While this medium can be an opportunity for a lot of good and positive activity, know that it also offers many opportunities for the flesh.

Does Social Networking Have a Positive Spiritual Impact on Self (1 Corinthians 6:12; 10:23-24)?

This might seem like an odd question to ask, but remember for every effect there is a cause. Everything in life has some kind of consequence. While technology might be neutral, it can't stay that way because the way we use it is imprinted by our worldview. How you utilize social networking will affect you one way or another. For example, if you belong to several groups or networks, and individuals in one of those networks communicate in a non-edifying manner, it is obviously going to have a negative impact. Probably the most destructive activities for any community are gossip and side hall conversations. If we're not careful, social networking will present opportunities to tear down or slander. Even if you aren't the one writing slanderous statements, you can be just as guilty for reading them.

Gossip is a billion-dollar industry that infiltrates websites, magazines, blogs, and television. We live in a culture that thrives on the misfortunes and dirty laundry of others. Some people make a living stalking celebrities, hoping to capture that one photo that will make them rich. Does reading about the divorce of reality-show parents or seeing pictures of domestic violence or dead pop stars build up in any way? As followers of Jesus, we are to be in the culture without being products of culture. While gossip is only one example of how social networking can have a negative spiritual impact, know it can destroy trust and relationships at the speed of now.

On another note, one of the fruit of the Spirit is patience. Yet patience is a foreign concept in this digital era. I am grateful that I can get the Internet anywhere, video chat with someone on the other side of the planet, and access billions of pieces of information in the blink of an eye.

But if we aren't careful, this technology can spoil us. The same luxuries that exist in the cyber world typically don't exist outside of it. For example, if you want to go from point A to point B, you still have to get in your car and drive there. I can travel thousands of miles away in the cyber world instantaneously, but that doesn't apply when I go out to dinner. We can't allow the luxuries we enjoy online to prohibit us from walking in the Spirit as we encounter situations that don't offer immediate gratification and might even require patience.

Will Social Networking Addict (1 Corinthians 6:12)?

I have friends who check their social-networking sites almost hourly. They can't go through a meal without posting what they're eating and who they're eating with. Their connection to the cyber world has become an addiction that consumes hours each day.

Like most things, social networking can but shouldn't become addicting. Remember, technology exists to serve us, not the other way around. It's a way to communicate, not a place to live your life. Consider the following statements on addiction:

- Saint Augustine: "Bound as I was, not with another's irons, but by my own iron will. My will the enemy held, and thence had made a chain for me, and bound me. For of a forward will, was lust made; and a lust served, became custom; and custom not resisted, became necessity. By which links, as it were, joined together (whence I called it a chain) a hard bondage held me enthralled."[2]
- C. S. Lewis: "If we consider the unblushing promises of reward and the staggering nature of the rewards promised in the Gospels, it would seem that our Lord finds our desires not too strong, but too weak. We are half-hearted creatures, fooling about with sex and drink and ambition when infinite joy is offered to us . . . We are far too easily pleased."[3]

I'm not comparing most online activities to lust, sex, or drinking alcohol. But did you catch the last part of each statement? Augustine said his bondage held him "enthralled" and Lewis said we are "far too easily pleased" with things of this world. Don't be enthralled or too easily pleased by the desire to constantly be in the know with everyone you are virtually connected with. Such addiction can numb a person to the daring adventure of following Jesus.

Does Social Networking Go Against Your Conscience (Romans 14:14)?

Maybe you are reading this and wondering what all the concern is about. Maybe you don't have an online profile, and you wonder if you're the only one. I'm certainly not pressuring you to spend more time communicating online. If something about having a social-networking account doesn't feel right to you, then simply carry on without one. No rule says you're better because you utilize this medium. In fact, we need to view such technology as a luxury that helps us accomplish a goal, not a goal itself.

I have a friend, a teacher, who used to be addicted to Internet pornography. It almost completely destroyed his life. God has restored him and his relationships, and he hasn't looked at porn in years. But to this day he doesn't feel comfortable having a computer in his office. Whatever work he needs to accomplish through e-mail and social networking, he does at a library where anyone can walk by and see what he's working on. While he might be free to have a computer in his office, his conscience won't allow him to do so. Our conscience can serve as a powerful tool when we are trying to make decisions on the gray areas of life. At times, your conscience could well be the last line of defense to keep you from making a decision you shouldn't.

Will Social Networking Disrupt Fellowship and Damage Relationships Within the Community (Romans 14:15)?

The digital era has redefined certain terms for us. Words like *friend* and *community* have been reduced to someone who might have no connection to us at all except that we accepted their friend request. On the other hand, our online "friends" can be individuals we do life with, work with, and worship alongside.

Let me ask you a couple of questions: First, do you think a biblical New Testament kind of community can exist solely online? Second, can authentic relationships form and grow online with no extra-virtual interaction?

Before I give you my answers, let's come up with a biblical definition of *friendship* and *community*. Here's one possibility: An inner circle of individuals who care for each other's souls as if they were their own, for the purpose of helping each other be rooted and built up in Jesus and established in the faith. The qualities of friendship are love (see 1 Samuel. 18:1,3), oneness (see Ecclesiastes 4:9-12), loyalty (see Proverbs 18:24), counsel (see Proverbs 27:9), kindness (see Job 6:4), honesty (see Proverbs 27:6), sacrifice (see John 15:13), obedience to Jesus (see John 15:14), communication (see Exodus 33:11), self-control (see Proverbs 22:24-25), and character (see Proverbs 27:17). While many of the qualities of friendship and community can be exercised online, they also require an intimacy and emotion that can't be experienced virtually. In other words, biblically defined relationships can't be downloaded, but they can be supported and experienced through social networking.

Will Social Networking Damage Your Reputation (Romans 14:16)?

The bottom line on this question is that your life is the sum total of the decisions you've made. If you express something out of anger without first thinking it through, then that statement potentially could damage your reputation. We live in a world that has the ability to record everything that happens and recall it at the most inopportune times. In a recent political campaign, one politician's daughter's boyfriend had made some damaging comments a year before the election. Of course, his comments were exposed in the campaign, and it damaged his reputation. The Bible teaches us to take our thoughts captive to the obedience of Christ (see 2 Corinthians 10:5). If you establish this discipline in your life, then your reputation won't be damaged through social networking. On the other hand, if you allow your thoughts and emotions to run wild, posting whatever comes to mind, you'll face a much different outcome.

As believers, we're wise to develop some guidelines for living a godly life on the Internet. Some parameters might include "Never post something you would be ashamed to say in a crowded room" or "Don't write what you wouldn't want repeated."

Will Social Networking Remove Focus from the Big Picture of God's Kingdom (Romans 14:17-19)?

How much time do you spend online each week? A couple of hours? Several hours? More than twenty? It's easy to lose track of time when you are virtually conversing with friends and getting the latest updates on what's happening in their lives. Nothing is necessarily wrong with keeping informed—after all, a good friend should know what's taking place in another friend's life. Yet we must guard our hearts against becoming obsessed with the trivial.

The kingdom of God isn't comprised of trivial matters, like vacation photos or what someone wore that day. Instead, God's kingdom consists of things that make for peace and are mutually upbuilding: "Your task is to single-mindedly serve Christ. Do that and you'll kill two birds with one stone: pleasing the God above you and proving your worth to the people around you" (Romans 14:18, MSG).

Social networking is a powerful tool that can help people focus on what God's kingdom is all about or distract them from the kingdom with meaningless chatter. You'll always face the challenge of rising above the white noise. Focus is never easy. The evolution of technology and the way we communicate can be used to serve others and represent Christ, but using it for the kingdom is a decision we must consciously make.

Does Social Networking Further the Advancement of the Gospel of Jesus Christ (1 Corinthians 9:19-24; 10:33)?

You are a missionary. Wherever you go and whatever you do, you bear the name of Christ. Social networking is a great door of opportunity to share the good news of Jesus with people who don't know him. Go back to your answer of how much time you spend in the cyber world each week. Now multiply that number by fifty-two. If you only spend two hours a week online (most of us spend much more), then in one year you will spend more than a hundred hours online. That's a lot of missed opportunities to have conversations about Jesus.

Questions from the "how to believe" grid are meant to help us chase down the elephants in our lives without losing sight of the goal. Remember, freedom in Christ has the goal of demonstrating Jesus even in the secondary issues of life so that others may be saved. In other words, even in secondary issues, freedom points to the primary goal of Jesus. When it comes to our online activities, the Internet should not be a place to escape, but to engage.

C. S. Lewis never knew what a computer looked like. But his words still apply when it comes to exercising our freedom in the cyber world while, as always, pairing it with responsibility:

> As Christians we are tempted to make unnecessary concessions to those outside the Faith. We give in too much. Now, I don't mean that we should run the risk of making a nuisance of ourselves by witnessing at improper times, but there comes a time when we must show that we disagree. We must show our Christian colours, if we are to be true to Jesus Christ. We cannot remain silent or concede everything away.[4]

CHAPTER 8

ELEPHANT 3: SOCIAL DRINKING

A few years ago I had the privilege of speaking at a church in Germany. Each night I preached an evangelistic sermon in the church, and I also spoke in more than thirty schools over the course of four days. It was an amazing time of seeing people cross the line of faith to accept Jesus as their Savior and Lord.

One of the more encouraging aspects of the week was the diversity of people who came and made decisions: old and young, rich and poor, homeless and home free, all coming to the level ground in front of the cross.

I stayed in the home of a very generous family who didn't speak a word of English. Most of the time we just looked at each other and smiled. On my final night there, in celebration for all that God had done, the husband went to a closet and retrieved what I think was some of his best and oldest wine. As he showed me the bottle, he managed a couple of statements like "God is good" and "Praise God." He lives in a culture, or at least a large part of the culture, that takes no issue with having a glass of wine or drinking a beer. I could give a hundred other examples from around the world of individuals who feel the same way.

Growing up, my church took a very different approach to this issue. Drinking alcohol was taboo. Kids in Sunday school came away convinced that wine in the Bible meant grape juice. To the teenagers, the message was simple: Alcohol is bad; only sinners drink.

Of course, this caused quite a bit of confusion for me personally when I discovered that some Christians, and even some ministry leaders, drank alcohol. It seemed Christians assumed that either it's okay to drink alcohol or it's bad. Either way, we're mistaken to make assumptions. The Bible teaches us to "test everything" (1 Thessalonians 5:21). That's the constant responsibility of every Christian, because we can never afford to become a product of culture; rather, God calls us to be the ones who create culture and see it transformed.

Before we go on, I want to say that this isn't a chapter about why you should or shouldn't drink. Rather, it's about how to use the "how to believe" grid to wrestle with this issue. You'll see how I've dealt with the issue of social drinking, but you might choose different questions from the grid, have different answers for those questions, or come to completely different conclusions. What's important is that you wrestle with the issue based solely on questions sourced in Scripture.

Those two words in 1 Thessalonians 5:21 — "test everything" — provide a great guide for understanding our freedom in Christ. In the absence of knowing how to believe, we'll be tempted to make decisions based on what our culture thinks. We can easily become puppets in the hands of pop culture, relying on the ideas of others.

The Old Testament figure of Daniel provides a great example of someone who refused to be a puppet. He was young when the Babylonians came to Jerusalem and waged war on his home city. Rather than being killed, he was taken as a slave and made the long journey back to Babylon. Upon arrival, he was placed in a system designed to reengineer the way he thought, acted, and worshipped. Yet while he was in captivity, the Bible says that "Daniel purposed in his heart that he would not defile himself with the portion of the king's delicacies, nor with the wine which he drank" (Daniel 1:8, NKJV). From this we gather that the dietary options given to him in captivity went against his Hebrew convictions. While Daniel could have taken the easier path, eating and drinking whatever he was given, he had a worldview or filter by which he tested everything.

That's the purpose of the "how to believe" grid we're using to talk about approaching some gray areas of life — the elephants in the room that most people just choose to ignore. For the first elephant, homosexuality, we focused on the question of what God's Word says about the issue. With the second elephant, the cyber world, we focused on how to operate within that medium, particularly in regard to social networking. Now we are dealing with an issue that will have a clear outcome: abstain or partake.

For the purposes of this discussion, we'll use the phrase "social drinking" to refer to casual drinking in a social setting without the intention of getting drunk. This would include situations such as having a glass of wine with dinner, drinking a beer while watching a game, or having an alcoholic beverage and talking with friends. Now let me state the obvious. As Christians, we are subject to governing authorities (see Romans 13:1-7). In the United States, our laws prohibit individuals from purchasing or drinking alcohol until a certain age. To argue that you are free in Christ to drink alcohol below any age restriction is to "resist the ordinance of God, and those who resist will bring judgment on themselves" (Romans 13:2, NKJV). So don't go there.

Finally, before we take the issue of social drinking through the grid, I'd like to add a precursor. Christians, even those considered strong in the faith, don't always agree. In fact, you might answer the questions that follow differently than I would. The point is not that you come to the same conclusions as I do, or even go on the same journey. The hope is that you'll have your own journey and come to your own conclusions. What should be the same for all of us is that we go to the same source, the words of the Bible. In doing so, we come away asking the right questions. Wherever you land on this issue, just make sure it's your conclusion. Be convinced in your own mind. What follows is how I was able to accomplish that in my life.

HOW TO BELIEVE: SOCIAL DRINKING

Is Social Drinking Within the Explicit Moral Will of God?

Of course, to arrive at an answer to this question about social drinking, we start with evaluating what the Bible has to say concerning alcohol and its consumption. We need to get an overview of how the Bible refers to alcoholic drink or wine.

Is this issue as simple as saying that when wine is mentioned, the

Bible is referring to grape juice? If that were true, then Scripture wouldn't include strong statements against drunkenness. After all, you don't get drunk on grape juice. Most of the time, wine in Scripture speaks of grape juice that has already fermented or at least begun the fermentation process. The Bible contains well over two hundred references to wine. The most common Hebrew terms in the Old Testament are *yayin*, usually translated "wine" and *Šhēhkār*, usually translated "strong drink."[1] The most common term for "wine" in the New Testament is *oinos*, and we find one use of *sikera*, which means "strong drink."[2] The New Testament contains fewer references to alcohol than the Old Testament. Overall, the Bible offers positive, neutral, and negative statements regarding the use of alcoholic beverages. In fact, of all the statements about alcohol in Scripture, there are far more positive and neutral statements than negative ones.

First, let's look at some of the neutral references:

- Genesis 14:18 refers to Melchizedek, a righteous king who was also a priest, offering wine to Abram.
- Nehemiah 2:1 talks about the king drinking wine. (Nehemiah was required to taste the wine first to make sure it was not poisoned.)
- Esther 5:6; 7:1-2 speaks of wine that Esther drank with the king.
- Job 1:13 refers to the family of Job (a righteous man) drinking wine.
- Daniel 10:3 speaks of drinking wine as a blessing after a time of fasting.
- Some of Jesus' parables are about wine, wineskins, and vineyards (Matthew 9:17; 21:33; in John 15, God the Father is called the vinedresser).
- Paul told Timothy to drink some wine (and not just water) for his stomach's sake in 1 Timothy 5:23.[3]

Second, here are some positive statements:

- Deuteronomy 14:26: "Spend the money for whatever you desire—oxen or sheep or wine or strong drink, whatever your appetite craves. And you shall eat there before the LORD your God and rejoice, you and your household."
- Psalm 4:7: "You have put more joy in my heart than they have when their grain and wine abound."
- Psalm 104:14-15: "You cause the grass to grow for the livestock and plants for man to cultivate, that he may bring forth food from the earth and wine to gladden the heart of man, oil to make his face shine and bread to strengthen man's heart."
- Proverbs 3:9-10: "Honor the LORD with your wealth and with the firstfruits of all your produce; then your barns will be filled with plenty, and your vats will be bursting with wine."
- Song of Solomon 1:2 compares love to wine: "Let him kiss me with the kisses of his mouth! For your love is better than wine."
- Isaiah 25:6: "On this mountain the LORD of hosts will make for all peoples a feast of rich food, a feast of well-aged wine, of rich food full of marrow, of aged wine well refined."[4]

I find it amazing to note how many positive statements connect wine to God's blessing and love. On the other hand, the Bible also contains several notable negative statements regarding wine that we'll look at in a few moments under other questions. But let's take a look at two passages here: Proverbs 23:29-35 and John 2:1-12.

Proverbs 23 provides one of the more vivid descriptions of intoxication in the Bible:

Who has woe? Who has sorrow?
　　Who has strife? Who has complaining?
Who has wounds without cause?
　　Who has redness of eyes?

Those who tarry long over wine;
>   those who go to try mixed wine.
Do not look at wine when it is red,
>   when it sparkles in the cup
>   and goes down smoothly.
In the end it bites like a serpent
>   and stings like an adder.
Your eyes will see strange things,
>   and your heart utter perverse things.
You will be like one who lies down in the midst of the sea,
>   like one who lies on the top of a mast.
"They struck me," you will say, "but I was not hurt;
>   they beat me, but I did not feel it.
When shall I awake?
>   I must have another drink.

The first half of verse 31 makes me pause: "Do not look at wine when it is red." The color red denotes a greater sense of strength, meaning the wine is further along in the fermentation process.[5] Israel's King Solomon, who wrote most of the wise sayings that comprise this book, is warning against the attraction of this alcoholic beverage and its appeal to our senses of sight and taste. He is saying that we must never become a prisoner to its enticing lure, but maintain our freedom against it.[6] He described the negative results of becoming entrapped by the allure of wine, including depression, self-pity, arguments, fights, babbling, and wounds from falling down. What's more, once a person caught in the attraction of alcohol gets sober again, he says, "Pass me another."

I realize that most explanations of this passage say that it describes individuals who draw comfort and security from knowing that a glass of wine is always at hand, ready to deaden their senses.[7] While this interpretation is likely true, it still gives me pause. As I have prayerfully chased this elephant in my own life, I've recalled this passage many times.

John 2:1-12 is the second notable passage of Scripture that casts a negative light on alcohol. In these verses, Jesus performed his first miracle, turning water into wine at a wedding at Cana in Galilee. Jesus and his disciples were invited to a wedding that his mother, Mary, was also attending. At one point during the festivities, the wine ran out. This was an embarrassing circumstance, so Mary turned to her son to find a solution. He responded by transforming the water in six large stone water pots to wine. This probably equaled between 120 and 180 gallons.

But did Jesus really create an alcoholic beverage? Apparently, because

When the master of the feast tasted the water now become wine, and did not know where it came from (though the servants who had drawn the water knew), the master of the feast called the bridegroom and said to him, "Everyone serves the good wine first, and when people have drunk freely, then the poor wine. But you have kept the good wine until now." (verses 9-10)

The master of the feast is like a host or head waiter. His comments are very telling. Most of the time, people would serve the best-tasting wine first, and once the guests' palates were numb — probably from the alcohol — they would bring out the cheap stuff. In the first century, one of the purposes of wine was to purify and give flavor to water, because water was usually retrieved from a well or cistern. A fairly common ancient ratio was three parts water and one part wine.[8] While it's possible to become intoxicated on this type of wine, you'd likely make a few trips to the restroom before reaching that state.

Please understand that I'm not dismissing the fact that Jesus made alcoholic wine. In fact, he made the best wine those people had ever tasted. Rather, we should take into consideration that the alcohol content in first-century wine might not be the same as the alcohol content in twenty-first-century wine. In fact, most everyone partook of the wine during that era, even children. I'm simply pointing this out so that we're careful not to say, "Jesus' first miracle was turning water into wine, so it must be okay to drink wine." It might not be that simple. Keep in mind that the purpose of the "how to believe" grid is to help us gain clarity by focusing on what the Scriptures teach. That's why I take historical, extra-biblical evidence into consideration, but I'm careful not to make it the central focus of my argument. Unfortunately, this is the approach taken by many who believe abstaining from alcohol should be required for all Christians.

As we survey the extensive landscape of what Scripture says about social drinking, there seems to be no strong statements prohibiting it. Therefore, in the absence of a definitive statement, social drinking becomes a freedom-in-Christ issue. That's why we need to ask the following questions.

Is the Decision to Socially Drink Being Made in the Attitude of Christ (Romans 15:1-13)?

The attitude of Christ is never about rights or a sense of entitlement. As we chase the elephants we're using as examples in this book, you've probably noticed that some issues are more sensitive than others. The issue of social drinking, no matter the perspective, seems to strike a nerve. Those who believe that all Christians should abstain are often quick to pass judgment, condemning others for enjoying what they feel are God's good gifts. On the other hand, some who partake immediately categorize the abstainers as weak and imprisoned by cultural tradition or even legalism. As we strive to have the attitude of Christ, our freedom should never lead to a place of condemnation. If that's the case, we've begun to misuse the sacred.

For my personal journey, I had to ask if social drinking improved my attitude in a Christlike manner, specifically in the areas of serving, building up community, and worship. You may be thinking, *Well, it doesn't help but it doesn't hurt, so this question isn't applicable to me.* I discovered that it was very difficult for me to have a Christlike attitude and partake in alcoholic beverages. That might not be true for you, but we don't have the same pasts. During high school and a few times in college, I abused alcohol. I drank, got drunk, and made a fool of myself. So for me, alcohol represents memories and mistakes, sins and sorrows. I can't help but associate it with my carnal flesh.

I believe this "attitude of Christ" question can be strategically helpful to all of us. Biblically informed thought combined with the right attitude can afford us great wisdom. What are your reasons for partaking or abstaining? Do your reasons represent the attitude of Jesus well?

Is the Decision Being Made Under the Control of the Flesh or the Holy Spirit (Galatians 5:13-26)?

In Galatians 5:19-21, the apostle Paul listed drunkenness as a work of the flesh. So, intoxication goes against a direct command from God. However, when it comes to social drinking (without the result of drunkenness), our flesh cannot be the reason for either partaking or abstaining. For example, if pride is a reason for either, then the decision is being made in the flesh.

I knew a man who felt that partaking of alcohol in moderation was part of enjoying his freedom in Christ. But he had a habit of going out of his way to be noticed and associated with alcohol. He would bring the subject up in conversations or position himself to be seen holding a glass of wine. One night, we were having dinner at a restaurant. When it was his turn to order, the first words out of his mouth were an attempt to order a mixed drink. But just moments later, he asked the server to bring him a soda. His flaunting of his freedom to partake was a pattern he eventually grew out of. Freedom doesn't flaunt. We shouldn't go out of our way to show people, "Look what I get to do," because it contradicts the central elements of freedom — particularly those that motivate us to serve others, build community, and live in a worshipful manner.

Only when we operate in the Holy Spirit, not the flesh, can we do the will of God. That's why I must ask, "Is social drinking a hindrance to doing the will of God?" For me, it can hinder — again, probably because of how I associate alcohol with past ungodly behavior. Still, I desperately want to live each moment in surrender to what honors God. On the other hand, I have friends who love Jesus and are strong in the faith, who drink wine with dinner. Knowing them well, I would testify to anyone that they walk in Christ and the fruit of the Spirit is evident in their lives.

Will Social Drinking Addict or Enslave (1 Corinthians 6:12)?

Freedom mishandled can make a god out of the elephants we chase. Addiction is a dangerous pitfall that has caused the destruction of millions. No matter what preconceived notions you have about social drinking, this question should make us think. Drinking can, although it certainly does not always, lead to alcoholism. While I've readily admitted that abstainers shouldn't falsely accuse partakers of abuse, with the same conviction we can't ignore the destructive possibility of what could be around the corner of one drink. Adrian Rogers, a great pastor who has gone home to be with Jesus, used to say, "Becoming an alcoholic does not begin with the last drink; it always begins with the first."

In chapter 6, we saw that the Bible doesn't condemn a homosexual inclination or orientation, and that just because someone has same-sex attractions doesn't mean he or she is immediately condemned. In the same way, some people are prone to alcohol addiction. For them, the first drink is the beginning of the end. Studies vary in telling us that a certain number of people who drink continue down the path to alcoholism; those who do succumb most likely have a genetic predisposition. So the logical question would be, "Who is or isn't genetically predisposed to this kind of addiction?" I've never seen any scientific evidence that can predict this condition.

As an exercise of the mind, let's say that number is one in twenty (most studies I read varied, so I rounded up). So if one out of every twenty individuals who takes a drink falls into addiction, at what point do the odds become justifiable? On the other hand, it's impossible to get bitten by a snake you never come in contact with.

Consider these biblical statements on drunkenness and addiction:

- Proverbs 20:1: "Wine is a mocker, strong drink a brawler, and whoever is led astray by it is not wise."
- Isaiah 5:11: "Woe to those who rise early in the morning, that they may run after strong drink, who tarry late into the evening as wine inflames them!"

- Isaiah 5:22: "Woe to those who are heroes at drinking wine, and valiant men in mixing strong drink."
- Luke 21:34: "Watch yourselves lest your hearts be weighed down with dissipation and drunkenness and cares of this life, and that day come upon you suddenly like a trap."
- 1 Corinthians 6:10: "Drunkards . . . will not inherit the kingdom of God."
- Ephesians 5:18: "Do not get drunk with wine, for that is debauchery, but be filled with the Spirit."
- 1 Timothy 3:1,3: "If a man desires the position of a bishop [elders and pastors] . . . [he must] not [be] given to wine" (NKJV).

Most of the forty negative references to alcohol in Scripture deal with abuse and addiction. These passages warn against abusing alcohol, provide examples of people who do abuse, and offer strict guidelines that church leaders should not be addicted.

The addictive potential attached to alcohol contributes significantly to my personal conviction. Pastor and author John Piper said, "Alcohol abuse is a great evil in our land. . . . I regard total abstinence generally as a wise and preferable way to live in our land today."[9]

Of course, I understand the argument that anyone can become addicted to just about anything: food, the Internet, sleeping pills . . . the list goes on and on. While it's true that all addiction is sin, it's equally true that not all sin bears the same consequences. For example, a shoplifter and a murderer don't receive the same punishment. Alcoholism can destroy relationships, work, and future possibilities. Some of the consequences are too overwhelming to even consider. Earlier we defined *addiction* as "a worship disorder"; what a tragedy it would be to bow at the feet of the god of wine.

Will Social Drinking Hurt a Brother Spiritually or Set a Spiritual Deathtrap (Romans 14:13)?

Hypothetically, the act of social drinking could cause a weaker Christian to stumble or even fall into a pit. As a church leader, I've counseled a number of weaker Christians about their struggle with alcohol who would be devastated if they saw me having a beer or a glass of wine. Remember, because they are weaker in their faith, I can't simply dismiss their feelings as petty or insignificant. I have a responsibility to them, part of which is to be patient with their weaknesses.

At the same time, I don't believe we can go through life constantly looking over our shoulder. Each individual is responsible for the knowledge he or she has. I can't make a dogmatic conclusion that Christians who have a drink publicly don't care about their brothers and sisters in Christ. To make this accusation, I'd have to be a mind reader (or the guy who writes what goes inside fortune cookies). But because I'm not, I refuse to cast judgment upon my friends—or any person—who choose to partake of alcohol in public. The point here is to <u>view your freedom through the lens of the rule for Christian living: that our lives would be dedicated in service to God and others.</u>

Does Social Drinking Go Against Conscience (Romans 14:14)?

Your conscience can guide or condemn. In either case, the Bible is clear that you can't ignore it. One of the struggles I experienced when chasing this elephant was that my conscience was guiding me toward abstaining. This raised some very serious concerns for me, because I didn't want to be weak in my faith due to rules and regulations that might not be from Scripture. However, when Paul discussed the weaker believer in Romans 14, he referred to someone imprisoned or even enslaved by traditions. I found this understanding very useful in keeping me from self-condemnation.

Not going against your conscience means you allow it to guide you in order to love God with all your being. John Piper made this statement, which helps as you consider the role of conscience in your effort to love God: "Freedom is more foundational than love. Inner freedom is the spring; love is the water that flows out in 'helpfulness' to others. The inner work of the Holy Spirit, freeing us from the enslavements of all but God, is the source of love."[10]

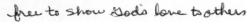
free to show God's love to others

Will Social Drinking Damage My Reputation (Romans 14:16)?
The answer to this question might depend on your relationships and culture. I've been given the great honor of helping lead an organization, Student Leadership University, that serves more than twenty-five denominations and movements each year as we teach students to think, dream, and lead. In addition, I also have the opportunity to speak in different parts of the country at a wide variety of events and experiences. Some days I'm with people who see social drinking as a complete non-issue. For them, not to have a glass of wine with a good steak is sin. On other days I'm with people who would take issue if they thought the guy on stage ever sipped an alcoholic drink. I don't ever want anything—like what I drink or don't drink—to stand in the way of anyone hearing a message. Certainly, at times I've been tempted to think, *If they have a problem, then they can just get over it; it's none of their business.* But a singular focus on Jesus should never allow such a thought to take root in my life. Paul said it this way:

> Even though I am free of the demands and expectations of everyone, I have voluntarily become a servant to any and all in order to reach a wide range of people: religious, nonreligious, meticulous moralists, loose-living immoralists, the defeated, the demoralized—whoever. I didn't take on their way of life. I kept my bearings in Christ—but I entered their world and tried to experience things from their point of view. I've become just about every sort of servant there is in my attempts to lead those I meet into a God-saved life. I did all this because of the Message. I didn't just want to talk about it; I wanted to be *in* on it! (1 Corinthians 9:19-23, MSG)

Can Social Drinking Be Imitated by Others Who Understand Their Freedom (1 Corinthians 10:33–11:1)?
Follow this thought: If a certain number of individuals who drink for the first time will become alcoholics, and it can't be known which individuals are genetically predisposed to such addiction, then how can I drink lest

someone imitate me and become addicted?

While you might not apply the same logic to this question, it's a thought worth considering. The main thrust of this question is that we do have a responsibility to others who understand what it means to be free. Paul was a leader among leaders, living an exemplary life that he could encourage others to imitate. I want that to be true of me.

At the beginning of this chapter, I told you our discussion of this issue wasn't about why you should or shouldn't drink. I don't believe it's right for anyone to be dogmatic concerning secondary issues. When it comes to these issues, the only thing I want to be dogmatic about is encouraging you to think for yourself, and providing you the necessary tools to do so.

If you haven't already figured it out, on the issue of social drinking I've chosen to abstain. I do so for what I believe to be healthy and God-centered reasons. While I have weighed extra biblical data in my decision—like the ratio of wine to water in first-century wine—these bits of information have not become the center of my argument. Instead, I hope that I've based my decision on questions formulated from Scripture.

If you read this chapter, think through and pray over these questions, and come to a different conclusion than I did, I have no problem with that. Just make sure you are convinced in your own mind. In the end, you need to chase down these elephants in your life so they don't become distractions or obstacles to more important issues—like advancing the gospel of Jesus.

CHAPTER 9

ELEPHANT 4: ENTERTAINMENT

Answer these two questions: What was the last movie you saw? What was the last sermon you heard? Most of us will remember more about the movie than we will about the sermon.

Entertainment is alive and well in America. Even in turbulent economic times, people still go to concerts and movies. Records are still broken at the box office on opening weekends, and people still wait through the night to be one of the first to see a movie. Gossip magazines and websites thrive because it's not enough to just see a movie; we want to know everything, "warts and all," about our favorite stars.

Why are we so attracted to the art form we watch on some type of glowing screen? Why do we remember some movies better than most sermons? Brian Godawa, a Christian who wrote the screenplay for the movie *To End All Wars*, said, "Great movies are like incarnate sermons. . . . Probably because they put flesh onto the skeleton of abstract ideas about how life ought or ought not be lived."[1]

For the purposes of exploring our freedom as believers in regard to entertainment, we'll focus on some of the more popular forms of entertainment in our culture: movies, television shows, and videos posted on the web. Thinking Christianly about what movies we'll see or what shows we'll watch seems to be a theological road that very few travel. Some Christians simply determine that such entertainment attacks the moral fiber of decency and should be avoided. In other words, Hollywood is bad and we should just stay away from it. And some Christians decide to make explicitly Christian movies. I have friends who have done this quite successfully, and I wholeheartedly applaud their work. Still, the fact remains that most of us don't have a filter that allows us to approach entertainment in a God-centered way.

Freedom in Christ helps and motivates us to engage our culture, including entertainment. I'm not an alarmist who believes a giant boycott of entertainment is the answer. But I'm also not a passive cultural glutton who thinks it's okay to check your brain at the theater door. In fact, I refuse to believe these are the only two options. The president of Cedarville University, Bill Brown, writes and speaks extensively on entertainment and worldview. He framed the issue of entertainment choices well by stating:

> This question is really part of the "Christianity and culture" conflict Christians have confronted for two millennia. There has never been an agreement on what course of action is most biblical. One approach calls for believers to withdraw from the worst of popular culture and refuse to dignify any value in non-biblical and anti-biblical cultural expressions. After all, it is argued, aren't we called to "come out of from them and be separate" (2 Corinthians 6:17, NIV)? Another approach is to uncritically assimilate entertainment into our lives, an approach that is theologically flawed but widely practiced.[2]

Unfortunately, many of us do suspend our beliefs when it comes to entertainment. We sit in front of a screen and allow the images to infect our thinking. But does it really make sense to shut down our worldview, sit back with a supersized heart-attack-waiting-to-happen bag of popcorn and gallon of soda, and just veg?

Consider this: God doesn't want you to ever shut off your brain and become passive. He wants you to be able to discern what you see and hear. Remember, Scripture says to "test everything."

Before working our way through the "how to believe" grid, it's important to note that our culture has always thrived on storytelling through a wide variety of mediums. Jesus constantly used storytelling (parables) in his ministry. In recent history, master storytellers include authors like C. S. Lewis, who wrote about other places, and J. R. R. Tolkien, who wrote about other times. Lewis probably had one of the more helpful views of story, which can be understood through how he defined myth:

> The heart of Christianity is a myth which is also a fact. The old myth of the Dying God, *without ceasing to be myth*, comes down from the heaven of legend and imagination to the earth of history. It *happens* — at a particular date, in a particular place, followed by definable historical consequences. . . . By becoming fact it does not cease to be myth: that is the miracle.[3]

For Lewis, myth was the great symbol that captured something universal about the human condition. The incarnation of Jesus is the only true myth because it was the only time that story came to life. In other words, the story of the Bible — God coming to earth and sacrificing himself for humanity — became the standard for story. For example, all ancient forms of religion have some type of sacrificial system, which is an attempt to reunite what was separated at the fall of man. Because of the story that God has told, all other stories have some meaning.

Consider the following two statements by Brian Godawa:

> We are creatures of story, created by a storytelling God, who created the very fabric of our reality in terms of his story. Rather than seeing our existence as a series of unconnected random events without purpose, storytelling brings meaning to our lives through the analogy of carefully crafted plot that reflects the loving sovereignty of the God of the Bible. . . .
>
> Stories do not exist in a vacuum of meaninglessness. Movies communicate prevailing myths and cultural values. And this cultural effect is far deeper than the excesses of sex and violence. It extends to the philosophy behind the film. The

way we view the world and things like right and wrong are embodied in the redemptive structure of storytelling itself.[4]

As you can see, because we are part of a story being told by a story-telling God, we are naturally drawn to stories. Televisions shows, movies, and online videos are the major forms of storytelling in our culture. And, yes, we are part of a culture saturated and even obsessed with entertainment. But my hope is that we would neither get lost in it nor retreat from it, but allow our freedom to instruct and guide our engagement.

HOW TO BELIEVE: ENTERTAINMENT

Are My Entertainment Choices Within the Explicit Moral Will of God?

While specific entertainment choices such as reality television, online videos, or R-rated movies aren't specifically mentioned in Scripture, the Bible does speak about entertainment venues such as feasts (see Genesis 21:8), weddings (see Matthew 22:2), the return of a wayward son (see Luke 15:23), dinner (see Genesis 43:16; Luke 14:12), and festivals and banquets (see Leviticus 23). Of course, the mere existence of these activities in Scripture provides little guidance when attempting to think Christianly about our entertainment choices today.

As we move forward, let's be clear that we are discussing debatable entertainment. Obviously, this differs from entertainment choices that place believers in a position of watching or participating in something that contradicts Scripture. That would be sin. The psalmist put it this way: "I will set nothing wicked before my eyes; I hate the work of those who fall away" (Psalm 101:3, NKJV). An example of entertainment that contradicts Scripture would include movies with heavy doses of sexual acts, violence, and profanity, because none of these offers redemption from evil. Yet even that definition might have some gray areas. A horror movie aimed at teenagers with the plot of a crazed serial killer or demon and full of sex is detrimental to the minds of its viewers. On the other hand, a war movie that portrays the realities of soldiers who are willing to sacrifice their lives for those who have no freedom offers a great deal of redemptive qualities. While both the slasher movie and the war movie might have equal amounts of violence, a very different message or worldview is being communicated. So how do we know the difference? That's the purpose of the "how to believe" grid. When we ask these questions, Scripture becomes a lamp unto our feet.

Are My Entertainment Choices Being Made Under the Control of the Flesh or the Holy Spirit (Galatians 5:13-26)?

There is an old saying that says, "The gravity of our depravity will always pull us down." Even though you are a new creation in Christ and are no longer slave to your sin, fleshly desires still exist. Ephesians 4:22 instructs that you still have to "put off your old self, which belongs to your former manner of life and is corrupt through deceitful desires." Each day we must decide which life we will feed — the new life in Christ or the old self enslaved to sin. The life we feed most is the one that wins.

At this point, it's fitting to address the phenomenon of reality television. Reality TV as we know it began in the early 1990s with MTV's creation of *The Real World*. This show took seven people from different backgrounds and placed them in the same house for several months to observe their interactions. Since then, reality television has exploded with shows like *Survivor, Dancing with the Stars, The Bachelor* . . . and the list goes on and on. Multiple cable networks are devoted solely to reality TV, and *American Idol* is one of the most popular shows on the planet.

What draws us to watch reality shows? What within us compels us to watch these programs? Think about it. We'll dedicate ourselves to watching shows where people find the love of their life in a short time even though we know that five minutes after the show is over, they will probably break up. Does the believability of the drama keep us watching? Or are we simply tired of watching scripted shows? Certainly part of the attraction is the opportunity to peek in on other people's misfortune, whether that involves eating maggots or finding a mate. All of us possess a carnal curiosity that wants to see someone fall flat on his or her face, figuratively and literally, on national television. Of course, some reality shows accomplish positive things. Some are dedicated to helping people raise their children, achieve a clean home, or even possess a home at all.

In any case, our fascination with reality TV makes a statement about what we value in our culture. And we do value it. The Emmys now give a statue to the best host of a reality-TV show. Again, I'm not saying that all reality shows are bad. In fact, many are competitions that display real talent. But even on *American Idol,* some of the highest ratings are episodes that feature the worst auditions.

Let's face it: In our culture, we value shock, the lack of talent, failure, and all the drama that accompanies these negative qualities. Maybe these things make us feel better about ourselves and our own weaknesses (although this seems like poor motivation for spending our precious free time). Or maybe the reality-TV genre just helps us escape our own reality. Either way, this mainstream form of entertainment is valued within our culture.

Carnal curiosity is nothing new. In Luke 10:25-37, Jesus told the story of the Good Samaritan—a story we've all heard dozens of times. A guy goes down a road between Jerusalem and Jericho and gets mugged and beaten almost to the point of death. A priest walks down the road and immediately passes him by. Then the passage says, "Likewise a Levite, when he arrived at the place, *came and looked,* and passed by on the other side" (verse 32, emphasis added). That he "came and looked" tells us that he didn't hurry on by when he saw this man bleeding on the side of the road. The Levite slowed down to gawk a bit. This same carnal curiosity is why many times we slow down when passing the scene of a car accident.

Again, this discussion isn't to convince you to eliminate reality TV from your definition of acceptable entertainment. Rather, it's to get you to discern if you're watching a particular show under the control of the Holy Spirit or the flesh. Keep in mind that many of the shows in the reality genre receive their high ratings because they so vividly demonstrate the works of the flesh:

repetitive, loveless, cheap sex; a stinking accumulation of mental and emotional garbage; frenzied and joyless grabs for happiness; trinket gods; magic-show religion; paranoid lone-liness; cutthroat competition; all-consuming-yet-never-satis-fied wants; a brutal temper; an impotence to love or be loved; divided homes and divided lives; small-minded and lopsided pursuits; the vicious habit of depersonalizing everyone into a rival; uncontrolled and uncontrollable addictions; ugly paro-dies of community. I could go on.

Would it surprise you that those words come from Galatians 5:19-21, as expressed in *The Message*? Remember, carnal curiosity is nothing new.

Will This Entertainment Choice Have a Positive Spiritual Impact on Me (1 Corinthians 6:12; 10:23-24)?

We need to see movies, TV shows, and online videos in the proper light: They are a conversation in images. Neil Postman was a writer and cultural critic who wrote an important book in the 1980s titled *Amusing Ourselves to Death*. In this book, he evaluated the decline of communication in an age of media. Although he was dealing primarily with the effect of televi-sion on culture, his statements are just as applicable to shared videos on the Internet. He wrote,

> Although culture is a creation of speech, it is recreated anew by every medium of communication — from painting to hiero-glyphs to the alphabet to television. Each medium, like lan-guage itself, makes possible a unique mode of discourse by providing a new orientation for thought, for expression, for sensibility.[5]

We live in a world of constant change. This has never been more obvi-ous than with technology. With the creation of new ways to communicate images comes new ways to think, express, and feel. The consumption of these images through new and exciting media should come with a caution I heard from Bill Brown, a writer on worldview and entertain-ment: "Video leads us to think of the world as objects, while words lead us to think of the world as ideas."[6] A conversation that takes place only in images will eventually lead us to a place where we don't think and we just absorb. In other words, we would be amusing ourselves to death.

God has given us a great gift in our imaginations. However, we also live in an age where hundreds of millions of dollars are spent creating the visually stimulating epic battle scenes of good versus evil. While these scenes are extremely entertaining, they are creative interpretations based on another's imagination. While I enjoy these productions, they should never replace the exercise of my own imagination. No matter how they make me feel or stimulate my thoughts, I have no excuse for not using my own mind.

I enjoy reading my kids stories. And either they enjoy hearing them or they are great actors for preschoolers. One night I was putting my son, Gabriel, to bed, and he asked me to tell him a story. At the moment I was either too tired or too lazy to go retrieve a book from the den, so I made one up on the spot. The next night when I went into his room at bedtime, I was prepared with several books to choose from. I asked, "Which one do you want Daddy to read to you?" You can probably guess what his response was. "I don't want those books. I want the story in your head."

As I retold the story I'd made up the previous night, Gabriel remembered the slightest details—and it wasn't even a very good story. It was the tale of a little boy who went fishing with his daddy and caught a fish that was so big it took two hands to hold. After they caught the fish, they sat on the dock and ate red candy, talked and laughed, and then went home. This second night, when I got to the part about eating candy, I forgot to mention that it was red. Gabriel, realizing I'd left out a very important detail, interrupted and reminded me that the candy was red.

C. S. Lewis said,

A child is always thinking about those details in a story which a grown-up regards as indifferent. If when you first told the tale your hero was warned by three little men appearing on the left of the road, and when you tell it again you introduce one little man on the right of the road, the child protests. And the child is right. You think it makes no difference because you are not living the story at all. If you were, you would know better. *Motifs*, machines, and the like are abstractions of literary history and therefore interchangeable: but concrete imagination knows nothing of them.[7]

Of course, Lewis had one of the greatest imaginations ever, and you only need to read THE CHRONICLES OF NARNIA to see it vividly demonstrated. But I wonder if he would have wanted his stories depicted in a movie? I'm sure he at least would have wanted us to read the book for ourselves, utilizing our own imaginations to envision what Narnia looked and felt like. Reading the words off a page forces you to create your own images and allows you to live the story with a childlike wonder.

You might be thinking, *What does this have to do with a positive spiritual impact?* The answer is everything. Out of all the ways God could have provided to experience and study his truth, he did so with words: "And the Word became flesh" (John 1:14). God wasn't bound by words; he chose to use them so that our imaginations could help us live the story.

All that to say, if a conversation in images is the only form of entertainment we know, then we surrender a God-given opportunity to experience more. Sure, God used images as well: "For his invisible attributes, namely, his eternal power and divine nature, have been clearly perceived, ever since the creation of the world, in the things that have been made. So they are without excuse" (Romans 1:20). But the point is that God gave us his special revelation through his Son and his Word.

When it comes to entertainment choices, many of us easily fall back to wanting rules to follow about what we should or shouldn't watch. So we invent or follow someone else's discrimination and make our decisions based on content, such as cusswords, sex, and violence. I've often heard the question, "Can a Christian see an R-rated movie?" There's a significant problem with the manner in which the question is framed. Our freedom in Christ doesn't motivate us toward the boundaries as defined by the Motion Picture Association of America. Don't allow the boundaries set by culture to determine the boundaries of your freedom. Culture is always changing, and the boundaries God has already set are steadfast. Even still, the goal of freedom isn't to stay within God-set boundaries; rather, it's to allow his boundaries to point us toward the center of his will for our lives.

I'm not saying that we shouldn't use practical helps to contribute to our decisions. Obviously, to make an informed decision, we need to be informed. Many tools are available to provide insight into the content of a movie without spoiling the plot. While evangelical organizations produce some of these tools, I've found one I like — www.screenit.com[8] — that isn't biased toward any particular worldview but just gives me the facts. No, I'm not a paid endorser of this site, just a regular subscriber. It provides a quick overview of the plotline and then gives an in-depth analysis of any questionable content including alcohol and drug use; blood and gross stuff; disrespectful and bad attitudes; frightening and tense scenes; guns and weapons; imitative behavior; jump scenes; scary, tense, and inappropriate music; profanity; sex and nudity; smoking; and violence.

Several years ago someone told me about this site, so I gave it a test run by looking up a movie I'd recently seen. I was shocked to discover how many and what type of cusswords had been said! I like that this site just gives me the facts about movies, and I can make my own decision utilizing the "how to believe" grid. In fact, here's how I shortcut the grid. Once I know about the content of a movie, I ask three little questions:

1. Will it build me up?
2. Will it profit me?
3. Will it help me personally?

From there, I can usually decide if a movie will have a positive or negative spiritual impact on me.

Do My Entertainment Choices Addict or Enslave (1 Corinthians 6:12)?

Our culture facilitates gluttony of all kinds, including entertainment. Cell phones have become places to watch movies, TV shows, and online videos. If I'm unable to get to my television set at the right time, I can digitally record or watch a program online within twenty-four hours. We can sign up to have the latest movies delivered right to our doors, providing a steady stream of new releases in our homes. More theaters exist than ever before, and most of the movies Hollywood produces are seen all over the world.

If all of those choices aren't enough, we can go to YouTube, the video-sharing website where users can upload and share videos. This site was created in early 2005 and bought by Google in 2006 for $1.65 billion! It's believed that more people watch videos on YouTube than go to the movies or watch TV.

The bottom line is that we are responding to new ways to consume media like monkeys during banana time at the zoo. Right now the top three most-viewed videos of all time on YouTube have well over 100 million views (a comedian dancing, a music video, and a guy biting his brother's finger.

I'm not saying that we shouldn't watch funny online videos or movies or TV shows. But we certainly shouldn't become obsessed with watching them. How much time do we lose in front of a screen each week consuming media? Answering that question and comparing it to the amount of time spent on other activities can be quite telling. Just as Paul set up the boundaries of freedom in Romans 14, we too should set boundaries on the amount of time we spend with these forms of entertainment.

Another way this medium can enslave or addict is if we allow the values portrayed in a movie or show to determine our own values. A healthier approach would be to watch through the lens of a biblical worldview with the idea that the story might help shape or build on an already existing foundation. A case in point is female beauty. As someone who speaks to students every week of my life, I can often tell what a young woman watches based on what she is trying to look like. Much of what is portrayed shows women who are half plastic and half woman, who spend more time working out than working. Oh yeah, and they never sweat. Of course, this creates completely unrealistic expectations, and more importantly, these women have nothing to do with biblical womanhood.

Certainly, looks are important (I think my wife is hot!). But what is on a screen shouldn't be the portrait young women aspire to. After all, the Proverbs 31 woman is much more attractive. We must guard against letting our thinking be imprisoned by a false reality. Let's allow the Bible to always define reality.

Will the Entertainment Choice Have a Positive Spiritual Impact on Fellow Believers and the Community (Romans 14:19; 1 Corinthians 10:23-24; Galatians 6:1-10)?

Robert Johnston, professor of theology and culture at Fuller Theological Seminary, notes: "The conversion of life into an entertainment medium is pervasive."[9]

One of the great examples of this has to be from *Schindler's List*. This 1993 film tells the amazing story of a greedy German businessman who became a humanitarian amid the terror of the Nazi regime in World War II. By turning his factory into a safe haven, Schindler saved the lives of 1,100 Jews who would have been gassed in a concentration camp. In a moving scene toward the end of the movie, Schindler has to leave the country because he's considered a war criminal. The Jews he rescued wrote and signed a letter with the hopes that the Allies would know all he had done for them. They also presented him with a gold ring made from the fillings of their teeth; on the ring they engraved in Hebrew a Talmudic saying: "Whoever saves one life, saves the world entire." While this emotional scene is etched in my mind, the story doesn't end there. At the time the movie was released, there were nearly six thousand descendants from the Jews Schindler had rescued.

In October 1996, Christoph Meili watched *Schindler's List* at his local theater. The twenty-eight-year-old man worked as a night guard at the Union Bank of Switzerland in Zurich. A few months after seeing the movie, he was making his rounds at work one night when he passed by the room where the paper shredders were located. There, he noticed a couple of large containers filled with old books. This struck him as odd, because he'd never seen the bank shred old books before. Upon further inspection, he discovered books containing records dating back to World

War II. Meili stuffed one of the books and a sixty-page document under his clothing and took them home.

Meili discovered that the book contained a ledger documenting Jewish-owned property that had been confiscated in Berlin and turned over to the Nazis. Remembering the movie and the scenes of the Nazis stealing from the Jews, and what Schindler had done, Meili was convinced that he needed to do something with the information he'd discovered. The next day, he returned to the bank to discover that the books had been shredded. But when he searched through the garbage, he found two of the books that were too large for the shredder. In an effort to go public with his findings, he contacted several media outlets. A Zurich newspaper put him off as did a Jewish organization saying, "This is dynamite—too hot to handle." A small Jewish newspaper finally ran the story, a press conference was held, and the story exploded worldwide.

Meili lost his job and received death threats. He was accused of being an Israeli spy and was investigated by police for stealing "bank secrets." Fleeing his country, he became the first Swiss resident in history to receive asylum in the United States.

Here's the point of this story: As a result of this one man, the Swiss banks had to reach a settlement with the Holocaust survivors, their families, and Jewish groups. The amount was $1.2 billion.[10]

Movies are a powerful medium that can have a positive impact on the culture. Meili was a Christian working a normal job; he saw a movie that reinforced an already existing value and inspired him to do the right thing. I have personally seen movies motivate service, compassion, patriotism, sacrifice, and political action. These entertainment choices have had a positive spiritual impact on the community of believers, and those outside the faith as well. Could entertainment become something that contributes to community?

Some churches have people watch movies as a group and then discuss the films. The goal of this is twofold. First, it helps believers think critically when watching movies. This helps people process things through their worldview and trace the idea of redemption by understanding the movie's theme, the hero, the hero's goal, the adversary, character flaws, apparent defeat, final confrontation, self-revelation, and the resolution.[11] In doing this, the viewer can engage the story without suspending the ability to think Christianly. Second, this creates open dialogue about what's right and wrong, and about what we should or shouldn't value. Such an exercise can have a positive spiritual impact and help build community.

Does This Entertainment Choice Go Against Conscience (Romans 14:14)?

I don't think it's an overstatement to say there are certain movies, TV shows, and online videos that no Christian should see. However, many others might be a matter of conscience. After gathering evidence and asking the right questions, there still might be a moral sense or voice of reason that watching a particular film or video will not help accomplish any of the goals of freedom.

The Greek word that the apostle Paul used for *conscience* is *suneidesis* (see Romans 2:15; 1 Corinthians 8:7,10,12). This word actually finds its origin in paganism, where it was meant to experience remorse for bad actions.[12] Paul expanded the definition of the term to also include the ability to direct or justify moral conduct.[13] I have chosen not to see some movies, and my reasoning has nothing to do with cussing, violence, or any sexual content but everything to do with the fact that my conscience wouldn't allow me. Dietrich Bonhoeffer, a great pastor and theologian who stood in opposition to the Führer, said, "The man with a conscience fights a lonely battle against the overwhelming forces of inescapable situations which demand decisions."[14]

Can the Entertainment Choice Be Imitated by Others Who Understand Their Freedom (1 Corinthians 10:33–11:1)?

A friend of mine went to a movie with a group of pastors. They wanted to see a particular film that he hadn't heard of. They found their seats, the lights dimmed, and the feature began. Within ten minutes, questionable content was on the screen, creating an awkward moment for the pastors. They looked at each other and, without saying a word, all were thinking the same thing. They quietly got up and left the theater. The reason was one of reputation and imitation. The movie didn't personally edify or build up.

While certain entertainment choices can contribute to community, others can be destructive. Whether an online video, movie, or TV show, we must always keep others in mind. Some Christians involved in entertainment dismiss this very idea, believing that the maturity of the audience should determine the type of content. However, maturity doesn't provide a free pass to take in excessive cursing, sexual content, and graphic violence. The significance of this question is that it constantly raises the bar of expectations and responsibility through being accountable to others.

I hope as you have walked through some of the questions in the "how to believe" grid that you understand how entertainment can contribute to community sometimes. Because of that, our freedom shouldn't motivate us to retreat, but to engage in a God-centered approach.

I enjoy movies, online videos, and even a rare good television show. Like it or not, these media are the most popular forms of storytelling and entertainment in our culture. The freedom we enjoy in Christ can serve us well so that we can enjoy these forms of entertainment without being amused to death.

CHAPTER 10

ELEPHANT 5: HUMANITARIAN EFFORTS

Recently, I was invited to lunch by an organization that wanted me to speak at its annual gathering of churches. It was a nice restaurant, in a nice part of town, so it only made sense to go. I don't remember much of the conversation or the meal. But something took place on the ride home that I'll never forget.

I pulled out of the parking lot in my air-conditioned SUV on a hot central Florida day and stopped at the first stop sign. Immediately, a woman struggling for breath on the side of the road caught my eye. She was a heavyset woman wearing a long dress, and sweat was pouring down her face. She was sitting with one hand on her chest as she gasped for each breath; with her other hand she motioned for me to roll down the window.

I did so, leaned my head out, and asked a dumb question: "Are you okay?"

Her response was heartbreaking. "No, sir. I've been sitting on this street corner for almost an hour. I'm having an asthma attack, and nobody will stop and help me."

I told her I'd give her a ride wherever she wanted to go. Before I could even open my door to help her, she stumbled across the street and got into my vehicle.

I turned on the AC full blast and asked where I could take her. The directions she gave me were only about three miles away. I asked her what had happened that she found herself having an asthma attack on a street corner during the middle of the day. This was the story she told me:

Last night, I came home from my job to find a big yellow lock on my front door. Now, the landlord is the only one I ever seen use that kind of lock. So I marched over to his office and asked him, "Why did you lock me out of my house? I paid you the rent!"

He responded, "Yes, but you are $26 short, and until I get my money, the lock don't come off."

Now, mister, I have three kids, and we don't live in the safest neighborhood. But last night we had to sleep on the front porch. This morning, I put my kids on the school bus and told them, "Don't you worry; by the time you get home, Momma will have the lock off that door." I came down here to ask if some businesses I used to clean for would loan me some money, but none of them would. One guy gave me some food, but food's not going to get the lock off my door. Now, mister, I have a job! I work hard to take care of my kids. But times are tough, and this month I guess I came up a little short.

When none of my former employers would loan me some money, I went to a church. But when they found out why I was there, they just called the police on me. They said it was illegal to ask for money in the city, but the police officer only wrote me a warning. I have it right here.

At this point, I was angry. And I don't mean "Acts 17–apostle Paul–righteous indignation" anger. There wasn't much righteous about what I was thinking. In my mind, it was time to call Jack Bauer or get Rambo out of the nursing home and, let's just say, have some fellowship.

You do realize what just happened: When the church called the police on "the least of these," the church called the cops on Jesus. Then, as I pulled onto the street where she lived, my mind and heart awakened to the reality that I was just as bad as the church that had called the police. This woman needed the love of Jesus, but I was taking her home to a locked house. She would have to look at her children that afternoon and explain how "Momma had let you down."

Without a word, I turned the vehicle around and began driving away from her house. She asked, "Uh, mister, where are we going?"

I explained that we were going where I should have gone in the first place—to the bank. I took $30 out, gave it to her, and began driving back to her street. She looked at the money, a twenty and a ten, and said, "Four extra dollars. I can feed my family for three days on $4." I asked her how that was possible, and she explained something about going to the butcher at closing time and boiling potatoes.

As we pulled up to her house, my heart sunk into my stomach as I realized I still hadn't done enough. I asked if I could help her some more by taking her to the grocery store. She smiled and said that wouldn't be necessary. Then she asked for my address so she could pay me back. She refused to accept any further help—help I should have given instead of casting judgment on others who had refused.

At times, we find ourselves living in a crazy, messed-up world that's full of hurt, hunger, and pain. Yet with all the need, we can still be reluctant to give ourselves away to the idea of service. We almost view service and love for those in need as something to be checked off a list.

But freedom demands much more. It demands that love become us, not merely be a part of us. It wasn't until I understood my freedom that I realized life is to be lived at the feet of Jesus. When I find myself at his feet, giving and going are something I do every day. They become me.

We live in a cause-driven culture. It seems as though every aspect of our society is baptized in one or more causes. You can buy a certain color cell phone, and a portion of your money will go to fight AIDS in Africa. You can buy a pair of shoes, and the shoe company will donate another pair to those in need in a third-world country. You can even buy cleaning products with the promise that the chemicals will not harm the environment. Whether your cause is green, red, or pink, I believe it to be a good thing. I applaud and am moved by the generosity of some people and organizations. Sure, some do it because it makes them look good or they want to convince us their product is trustworthy. But who cares, as long as people are being helped.

That isn't true, however, for those of us who follow Jesus. The right motivation is essential to serving Christ well. Our goal isn't merely to feed the hungry or put a roof over a homeless family. Rather, we serve with the hope that people will see Jesus in our generosity. Our freedom should motivate us to serve with the understanding that people have both visible and invisible needs.

For much of my ministry, I've sought and encouraged others to seek to do great things for the glory of God. I admit that I didn't think too highly of people who didn't share this persuasion. I honestly thought that if someone didn't want to do something great, he or she lacked vision and passion. However, after studying faithful men and women of God throughout history (and coming into contact with a few in my own journey), I'm now convinced that I may have been wrong for this simple reason: Greatness and great sacrifice often go hand in hand. I'm now convinced that a call to greatness might fall short of the mark. Instead, a call to serve would be a much more Christlike way to go.

So, I kicked greatness to the curb and began to discover something much more fulfilling: social justice, humanitarian efforts, march for this, and wear a wristband for that. The kind of service I'm talking about goes by different names, but I simply refer to it as "the Jesus thing."

I pray this chapter will challenge you to go forth and serve in his name, motivated by the freedom he has given you. Mother Teresa might have said it best when she said, "We can do no great things; only small things with great love."

HOW TO BELIEVE: HUMANITARIAN EFFORTS

What Is the Moral Will of God Concerning Humanitarian Efforts?

Of course, we'll begin building our case by asking if the Bible has any explicit statements on the issue of humanitarian efforts. And we'll discover that the Scriptures have quite a bit to say concerning this subject.

We noted earlier that if we can answer this first question by quoting chapter and verse in the Bible, then there's no need to go any further.

With the issue of homosexuality, the first question is as far as we went. The chapters on the Internet, social drinking, and entertainment required many questions from the "how to believe" grid.

Interestingly, with the humanitarian-effort elephant, we'll find that the answer to the first question is more than sufficient. Yet, in answering this question, we'll also answer several other questions in the grid, including:

- Is the decision being made in the attitude of Christ (see Romans 15:1-13)?
- Is the decision consistent with the rule for Christian living?
- Can the decision be imitated by others who understand their freedom (see 1 Corinthians 10:33–11:1)?
- Is the decision being made in light of the cause of evangelism (see 1 Corinthians 9:19-24; 10:33)?
- Will the decision glorify God (see 1 Corinthians 10:31); will the decision make a big deal about Jesus (see Galatians 6:11-16)?

Surprised by Grace

God's attitude toward this entire issue is quite clear in Matthew 25:35-40:

I was hungry and you fed me,
I was thirsty and you gave me a drink,
I was homeless and you gave me a room,
I was shivering and you gave me clothes,
I was sick and you stopped to visit,
I was in prison and you came to me.

Then those "sheep" are going to say, "Master, what are you talking about? When did we ever see you hungry and feed you, thirsty and give you a drink? And when did we ever see you sick or in prison and come to you?" Then the King will say, "I'm telling the solemn truth: Whenever you did one of these things to someone overlooked or ignored, that was me—you did it to me." (MSG)

We can sum up God's attitude as follows: A failure to serve the least of these is a failure to serve God. If we are truly free in Christ, then it should be evident in our lives by the way we interact with a world full of needs.

Two ideas need further explanation to understand God's attitude on this issue as demonstrated in this passage. First, people have needs that are very real and very obvious: hunger, thirst, homelessness, insufficient clothing, sickness, and imprisonment. Unlike some of our causes that might come and go, these needs have existed in every culture throughout time and history. These people are "the least of these," the obviously overlooked. What they need is what we all need: food, shelter, and companionship. By the very nature of these needs, we should immediately see that meeting them isn't something we can outsource or engage only on occasion. Freedom motivates and guides us toward building community, so an essential part of meeting these needs would be to graft "the least of these" into our communities. Serving in this way doesn't need to be accompanied by images of grandeur. Rather, it's one person inside one church meeting the needs of another.

I'm a Mother Teresa fan. I can't help it. It doesn't matter if all of our beliefs match up in just the same way or whether or not we would interpret certain Scripture the same. That's all irrelevant because she lived what mattered most: Jesus. Expressing his love isn't just something she *did*. It was something she *became*. She was known by the love of Jesus. At times, she didn't seem human; how could one human be so kind, so loving, care so much for those who had nothing? It was as if a tear from God himself had fallen from heaven, carrying a little Catholic nun in a faded blue sari and worn sandals. For her to love the poor was "the call within the call," and in doing so she exemplified to much of the human race a practical demonstration of Christ's command, "Love your neighbor."[1]

Mother Teresa met many of the needs described in Matthew 25:35-36. During an interview, she was asked, "What motivates you to perform the extraordinary works of charity for which you've become famous?"

She replied, "Ours is not a social work. We work twenty-four hours a day to express God's love. We evangelize by showing God's love. It is only through God's love that the poor can have their needs met."[2] Over the years she made so many of those profound statements with a sacred simplicity. While I can't cite them (I wrote many in my journals and on loose sheets of paper), I believe a few of them will help here:

- "The meaning of my life is the love of God. It is Christ in his distressing disguise whom I love and serve."
- "That is what I am. God's pencil. A tiny bit of pencil with which he writes what he likes."
- "If you can't feed a hundred people, then feed just one."

She believed poverty was really just Jesus in disguise. She believed in loving exhaustively—loving until it hurt—and knowing that if you did, you wouldn't discover hurt but more love.

My point isn't that you need to trade in your jeans and T-shirt for a sari and sandals, but that we are responsible to those in need. Our freedom demands it of us, and the example of Mother Teresa shows us the invincible weapon of God's love against the evils of this earth.

The second idea needing further explanation is noting that in Matthew 25:37-39, the righteous were surprised by what they heard. They didn't remember seeing Jesus or ministering to his needs. But as Mother Teresa pointed out, Jesus is often disguised in the least of these.

In fact, that points to the singular focus of the Christian life. When we operate in love, Christ is both the object and the recipient of our affections. This is supported by Scripture, which doesn't tell us that they hungry, thirsty, homeless, cold, sick, and imprisoned gave any response. Were they grateful? Did they also find salvation? Were they ungrateful?

What I'm about to say might sound a bit heartless at first. But could it be that the response of those in need is irrelevant to whether we should serve them? A laser-like focus on Jesus guards our heart from deciding who should or shouldn't have their needs met. The silence of their response in this passage speaks loud and clear to me. I am not judge and jury.

I realize this goes against much of how we raise money and motivate people to serve. Typically, we show a video that focuses on a need, followed by a plea of how to help meet that need, and finally an image of how happy people will be when you meet their needs. Don't get me wrong. People should be grateful, and there's nothing wrong with feeling a sense of accomplishment when you help meet the needs of hurting people. However, just know the attitude of Christ doesn't depend on the attitude of others. Shouldn't it be enough to see a need in our city or on the other side of the planet and say, "I'll go and give because going and giving has become me. Jesus is enough."

If you think that sounds topsy-turvy, consider another provocative statement from Jesus.

Pride, Prejudice, and Impossible Love

In his most famous sermon, Jesus spoke of love as essential Christianity in action. In Matthew 5:43-48, Jesus said,

> You have heard that it was said, "You shall love your neighbor and hate your enemy." But I say to you, Love your enemies and pray for those who persecute you, so that you may be sons of your Father who is in heaven. For he makes his sun rise on the evil and on the good, and sends rain on the just and on the unjust. For if you love those who love you, what reward do you have? Do not even the tax collectors do the same? And if you greet only your brothers, what more are you doing than others? Do not even the Gentiles do the same? You therefore must be perfect, as your heavenly Father is perfect.

In these few sentences, Jesus set the record straight on Christian love. One of the great themes of freedom in Christ is that we're not motivated toward boundaries; rather, boundaries help guide us toward a God-centered life. We shouldn't be motivated by how the person we help will respond, but out of our love for Christ. If we care more about a thank you or recognition, then we're missing the point. Because Jesus is enough, someone's nationality, political party, sexual orientation, color, or anything else is irrelevant. No matter what pride or prejudice we have, we are to love even our enemy.

There are two approaches to love that we must avoid. <u>First, we must avoid a segregated approach to love.</u> If you study the ministry of Jesus, one conclusion you can draw is that he was in no way intimidated by the religious establishment. The phrase "you have heard it was said" meant that the audience had heard the Pharisees (who were probably in the crowd) say such things. Jesus was calling them out for mishandling the law of love (see Leviticus 19:18) and turning it into a license to hate. Some Pharisees went as far as to teach that by hating those who were against Israel, you were helping God's judgment. There's only one big problem with this: The Old Testament law never commands you to hate your enemies. Jesus was saying that even though you've heard it, you've heard wrong.

<u>A segregated approach to love is one of limitations.</u> God hadn't chosen to love Israel and withdraw his love from the rest of the world; rather, He had chosen them to demonstrate his love to the whole world. *God's love can pour out of me to others.*

When I was in elementary school, we played a game called kickball. It's simple really. The field is set up as a baseball diamond, and the rules are similar as well. After three outs the teams switch, and if you could run around the bases without getting out, you score. The major exception is that instead of a baseball and a bat, you had a big red rubber ball that was rolled toward home plate and "the batter" kicked it.

Every day, when the recess bell rang, kids would flee their classrooms for thirty minutes to run free from spelling and math. Of course, only moments after the bell rang, a gathering would take place on the kickball field to divide into teams. Of course, for some kids, this can be a tense time that results in embarrassment and low self-esteem. Why? Because nothing is more feared in the minds of some children than being the last person chosen for playground games.

My situation was constantly on heightened alert because of a little girl—if you could call her that—who had to constantly prove she could play with the boys. One day, when just the two of us stood there after dozens of kids had already been chosen, I was mortified. To make it worse, a debate of pros and cons ensued by the choosing captains in an effort to make their decision. Alas, she was chosen first, and I stood there alone. I felt like one of those items on a salad bar that is always there but everybody passes over. Or maybe the fish sandwich at a fast-food restaurant; it's always on the menu, but no one ever orders it.

It's crazy to think we could actually segregate the love of God. Life isn't a game, and the idea of choosing who gets to be loved or where they get to spend eternity, is a task too incomprehensible for the human mind.

The second approach to love that Jesus warned us to avoid involves looking for an easy way to show love. It only seems natural to want to love people we'd enjoy spending time with. In fact, when teams were chosen for kickball, those who were friends of the captains got picked first. To love only those who love you is easy and comes naturally. But we're called to more. Jesus said that even the tax collectors could pull off that type of love. That might not sound like a big deal now, but in Jesus's day, a tax collector was a renegade Jew who worked for the Roman government collecting taxes against his countryman. He would often collect over the required amount in order to make money off his own people. Because of this, tax collectors were a despised group, and the Jews ranked them in the same lot as prostitutes. Jesus was saying that even men who are extortionists and traitors to their own nation love those who love them. To love those who love you is something that even the most morally corrupt can do.

After warning of these two approaches, Jesus offered a new standard. He contrasted the statement "You have heard" with "I say." Throughout all of history, prophets would proclaim, "Thus says the Lord." But Jesus' statement required no authority because he was his own authority.

The Greek language has four primary words for love. The first is family love, describing the love between a parent and a child. The second is sexual love, meaning the passion of human love and the desires between husband and wife. The third is affectionate love, which describes close friendships. But when Jesus said, "Love your enemies," he used the word *agape*. This word indicates unconquerable benevolence, invincible goodwill.[3] It means that no matter how I'm treated—whether I'm insulted, grieved, or injured—I won't allow bitterness and anger to invade my heart. In fact, I will seek the highest good for the person who has committed actions toward me. *God love*

Let me dispel any notion that God wants us to love our enemies as we would our family, a lover, or our closest friends. Rather, he wants us to love in a different kind of way. These first three types of love are all loves of the heart: We can't help but love our children, fall in love with our spouse, and be affectionate to those who are closest to us. These come naturally to us. But an agape love is one of both the heart and the will. It's not as much a feeling of the heart as it is a determination of the mind. This love is only possible when Jesus enables us to conquer our natural tendency toward anger and bitterness. I call it an "impossible love" because, left to our own determination, strength, and tendencies, we'd be unable to love our enemies. In fact, we'd have no reason to love our enemies because, left to our own desires, the flesh will always win and love will always lose.

Impossible love means that when God's love enters my heart and springs up, it drives out pride and prejudice. Agape love enables us to meet God's standards through the redemptive work of Christ, rather than him accommodating our human inadequacies (see 2 Corinthians. 5:21). As we look around, the world might seem at times like a sea of tears constantly fueled by tragedy. Making a difference might appear to be an impossible task. And it is. That's why we've been given an impossible love.

Freedom as Essential to the Movement of Christianity

I believe Christianity is a movement. A good analogy to help us understand this concept is a river that's concise, swift-moving, and flowing in a determined direction. The river can accomplish all this because of the stability offered by its banks. In other words, the banks facilitate all of the activity of the river. I believe that like this river, Christianity is a force. It has a source, Christ, and through the Scriptures and the church, it has a concise and determined direction. As the church, we are to facilitate the movement of Christianity based on the parameters taught in Scripture so that we can move toward the goal of Jesus. At the end of the day, Jesus is both the source and the goal of the Christianity movement.

To accomplish all this requires a clear understanding of freedom and how it motivates us to:

- Have the attitude of Christ
- Walk in the Holy Spirit
- Avoid the worship disorder of addiction
- Serve
- Build up our brothers and sisters in the faith
- Listen to our conscience
- Build community
- Have a godly reputation
- Never lose focus of the big picture of God's kingdom
- Lead others to Jesus
- Glorify God with every decision we make

All these components are embodied in the two texts that we've focused on in this chapter. And again, this is why answering the first question in the "how to believe" grid was sufficient. After all this, if we remain unengaged in efforts to serve the needs of others, we must ask ourselves if we're really operating within our freedom in Christ.

We can find many examples of people caring for the least of these in our world. One of the most recognizable names is the lead singer of U2, Bono. My reason for mentioning him will become evident in a few moments.

In February 2006, Bono was invited to address the National Prayer Breakfast, an annual gathering of almost four thousand religious and political leaders. Bono began his twenty-one-minute, forty-one-second speech by addressing the elephant in the room: "If you're wondering what I'm doing here, at a prayer breakfast, well, so am I. I'm certainly not here as a man of the cloth, unless that cloth is leather."

He explained how most of his life he had tried to avoid religious people. He had even referred to some television preachers as "God's second-hand car salesmen on the cable TV channels, offering indulgences for cash." Then he met a couple of British Christians who ruined his shtick, because they had the audacity to see the millennium as the Year of Jubilee, in which all the chronic debts of the world's poorest would be canceled. Bono continued,

> The church was slow but the church got busy...
>> Love was on the move.
>> Mercy was on the move.
>> God was on the move. . . .
>> God may well be with us in our mansions on the hill . . . I hope so. He may well be with us as in all manner of controversial stuff . . . maybe, maybe not . . . But the one thing we can all agree, all faiths and ideologies, is that God is with the vulnerable and poor.
>> God is in the slums, in the cardboard boxes where the poor play house . . . God is in the silence of a mother who has infected her child with a virus that will end both their lives . . . God is in the cries heard under the rubble of war . . . God is in the debris of wasted opportunity and lives, and <u>God is with us if we are with them</u>. . . .
>> It's not a coincidence that in the Scriptures, poverty is mentioned more than 2,100 times. It's not an accident. That's a lot of airtime, 2,100 mentions. [You know, the only time Christ is judgmental is on the subject of the poor.] "As you have done it unto the least of these my brethren, you have done it unto me."[4]

Bono's message primarily focused on AIDS and treatable diseases. along with equality and justice for the African people. He has carried his message to political and church leaders all over the world.

Now, I would in no way argue that Bono is the great portrait of freedom in Christ. After all, I don't know his heart. But I do know that he influenced Justin, a good friend of mine who heard Bono speak at a conference for church leaders in Chicago. After hearing Bono, God convicted Justin's heart, and he decided to take a trip to Kenya. He went with one penetrating question on his mind and heart: "How would my freedom motivate me to serve the movement of Christianity in east Africa?" While there, Justin realized that in order to see someone's life transformed, their physical needs must be met alongside their spiritual needs. For Justin, there was no tension between the two. Going and giving is not something Justin does; it's something he has become.

Today, I am proud to say that my friend Justin Miller has started an organization called CARE for AIDS. CFA seeks to mimic the holistic ministry of Christ in order to transform a community and empower the local church to offer help and support to people who have HIV/AIDS. They have centers in Kenya funded in partnership with American churches. They're helping many who have this terminal disease to realize that AIDS doesn't have to be the end of their story. This is the type of activity freedom in Christ motivates. For all of us, freedom in Christ is the door of opportunity to doing something significant for the kingdom.

A failure to serve people in need is a failure to serve God and a failure to live free. When we do serve, we might face impossible odds and obstacles, but we have the impossible love of Jesus on our side. John Chrysostom, considered the greatest preacher ever heard in a Christian pulpit, said, "It is foolishness and a public madness to fill the cupboards with clothing and allow men who are created in God's image and likeness to stand naked and trembling with the cold so that they can hardly hold themselves upright."[5]

I close this chapter with a question (surprise, surprise): Are you vulnerable to allowing God to break your heart over those who need food, shelter, companionship, or even have an incurable disease?

We live in a cause-driven culture, and we must be careful that others' needs don't become like the flavor of the month. We must guard ourselves not to become numb to it all. People in third-world countries or just down the street can be like the last movie we saw — we watched, and when it was over, we got up and walked away. But freedom doesn't leave us the option of walking away or even slowing down until the movement of Christianity has intersected with every spiritual and physical need on the planet.

After all, it's not a red, pink, green, or any other thing; it's simply the Jesus thing.

GRACE DEMANDS MORE

An exploration of freedom in Christ leads to one conclusion: The grace extended to me by God demands an exhaustive response. In other words, grace always demands more, never less.

When I use the word *demands*, I don't mean some dogmatic "my works can earn God's grace" type of way. Rather, after evaluating some of the primary biblical writings, extracting the goals of freedom, putting them into the form of questions, and then applying those questions to some elephants in the room, we can only come to one conclusion: *Grace demands more.*

This freedom guides us through secondary gray issues, affording us the opportunity to live with confidence and clarity. This clarity helps us focus on the primary issues—the things that matter most: God and Christian living. Freedom facilitates and ensures that in an ever-changing and chaotic world, we can stay at the feet of Jesus.

It's a strange thing being in the culture without becoming a product of it, living the present day rooted in what matters for eternity. In a way, freedom in Christ helps us create culture that glorifies our Lord. But no matter how you look at it, we are out of place. I guess that's because we are destined for another place. John Bunyan wrote of this in *Pilgrim's Progress*, saying that we are pilgrims on a journey to the celestial city. Our freedom keeps us from getting bogged down along the way.

One of my all-time favorite books is *All I Really Need to Know I Learned in Kindergarten* by Robert Fulghum, who has written eight best sellers with more than 16 million copies of his books in print. His kindergarten book is basically a collection of reflections on life as the author sees it. In it, he told a story of leading a game called "Giants, Wizards, and

Dwarfs" with eighty seven- to ten-year-olds in the church fellowship hall.

The purpose of the game is for the children to run around making a lot of noise and chasing each other until nobody knows what side they were on or who won. After organizing the room into groups, everyone was positioned and ready to go. Fulghum shouted one final instruction: Decide whether you are a Giant, a Wizard, or a Dwarf. He described what happened next:

> While the groups huddled in frenzied, whispered consultation, a tug came at my pants leg. A small child stands there looking up, and asks in a small, concerned voice, "Where do the Mermaids stand?" . . .
>
> A *very* long pause. . . .
>
> "There are no such things as Mermaids."
>
> "Oh, yes, I am one!"
>
> She did not relate to being a Giant, a Wizard, or a Dwarf. She knew her category. Mermaid. And was not about to leave the game and go over and stand against the wall where a loser would stand. She intended to participate, wherever Mermaids fit into the scheme of things. Without giving up dignity or identity. She took it for granted that there was a place for Mermaids and that I would know just where. . . .
>
> What was my answer at that moment? Every once in a while I say the right thing. "The Mermaid stands right here by the King of the Sea!" says I.
>
> So we stood there hand in hand, reviewing the troops of Wizards and Giants and Dwarfs as they roiled by in wild disarray.
>
> It is not true, by the way, that mermaids do not exist.
>
> I know at least one personally.
>
> I have held her hand.[1]

While the world seems to hurry by in a wild disarray, at times resembling eighty children running around a church fellowship hall, understanding our freedom allows us to stand without giving up our dignity or identity. When culture calls for you to be known as a republican or democrat, partaker or abstainer, red or green, Giant, Wizard, or Dwarf—and none of the categories seems to fit—please don't be alarmed. Your place is next to the King of the universe. And there you are free.

GRACE DEMANDS

Grace demands all of the components we've extracted from the sacred words of the Bible. By its very nature, grace leaves no other option. So with this closing section, we ask no more questions but offer a few concluding ideas about freedom and those who kneel before the King of the universe. Let's consider the following qualities that grace demands.

The Attitude of Christ

There's an old saying that comes across as cheesy. I mean, it sounds like it should be on a calendar in a nursing home. Anyway here it is: "Your attitude will determine your altitude." I hate it when cheesy sayings are true, because it totally challenges my prejudice against bumper stickers. That aside, my attitude is my decision. At the end of the day, life is 10 percent what happens to us and 90 percent how we respond to it. Your attitude is the single most important decision you'll make each day.

When it comes to freedom, our attitude can be like a flashlight revealing wrong motivations. John Maxwell, a leadership expert, speaker, and author who has sold more than 13 million books and whose organization has trained 2 million leaders worldwide, wrote of the importance of attitude:

> What is an attitude?
> It is the "advance man" of our true selves.
> Its roots are inward but its fruit is outward.
> It is our best friend or our worst enemy.
> It is more honest and more consistent than our words.

It is an outward look based on past experiences.

It is a thing which draws people to us or repels them.

It is never content until it is expressed.

It is the librarian of our past.

It is the speaker of our present.

It is the prophet of our future.[2]

In other words, Maxwell is telling us that attitude is one of the most important decisions of our lives. It determines so much of our existence. Yet we can take comfort in the fact that freedom in Christ can fuel and compel us to have the attitude of Christ.

A Spirit-Controlled Life

The works of the flesh are like spiritual rot, and addiction is the decomposition of our intimacy with Christ. When we give our lives to Jesus, the Holy Spirit indwells us. At that moment of salvation, we received all of the Holy Spirit that we're ever going to get. But there's a difference between indwelling and controlling. To be filled with the Holy Spirit means that the Holy Spirit controls you. Therefore, it's not a matter of how much of the Holy Spirit you have, but how much of you does the Spirit control. Understand that this involves a daily, moment-by-moment yielding to the control of the Spirit in all areas of our lives.

Boundaries

Martin Luther King Jr. is one of the more important figures in our culture in the last hundred years. He possessed the rare ability to communicate deep thoughts to a broad audience. He was brilliant. At a church conference in 1962 in Nashville, Tennessee, he addressed the idea of freedom and boundaries:

Neither am I implying that there are no limits to freedom. Always freedom is within a predestined structure. Thus a man is free to go north from Atlanta to Washington or south from Atlanta to Miami. But he is not free to go north to Miami or south to Washington, except by a long round-the-world journey; and he is not free to go to both cities at one and the same time. We are always both free and destined. Freedom is the chosen fulfillment of our destined nature.[3]

One who lives his or her freedom does not press up against the boundaries, always concerned with what may be on the other side. That person is confident that what is on the other side can in no way match up to what exists within the boundaries; if it did, God would have put it inside. The reason there are boundaries is so that we may live a God-centered life, a life in harmonious and even conversational intimacy with him.

Test Everything, Assume Nothing

In the preceding chapters, I made a big deal about testing everything and assuming nothing. In many ways, that's the purpose of this book. As I have studied Scripture and the lives of those who understand their freedom, I made the following comparisons. Look at the difference between people who live on assumptions and those who test everything:

People living on an assumption have busy and cluttered lives; people who test everything can't take their eyes off Jesus.

People living on an assumption know a lot but experience little; people who test everything see knowledge as a gateway to experience.

People living on an assumption follow lists; people who test everything follow Jesus.

People living on an assumption wander in a world of smoke and mirrors; people who test everything know that Christ offers confidence and clarity.

People living on an assumption are frantic; people who test everything are focused.

People living on an assumption will criticize and tear down; people who test everything edify and build up.

People living on an assumption are survivors; people who test everything are more than conquerors.

People living on an assumption have their agendas; people who test everything realize God blesses his agenda.

People living on an assumption live in culture; people who test everything create culture.

People living on an assumption serve out of duty; people who test everything serve out of delight.

People living on an assumption are lost in a crowd; people who test everything are alive in the marvelous light of Jesus.

I want the descriptions of those who test everything to be true of my own life. I hope you do as well.

A Clear Conscience

We let our kids watch some television. They have a particular fascination with Disney classics, and one of their favorites is *Pinocchio*. This 1940 film about a living puppet with a cricket for a conscience won two Oscars. But did you know that Pinocchio first appeared in the 1883 Italian novel for children titled *The Adventures of Pinocchio*?

The original story begins with a man named Mastro Cherry, who wants to carve a pine log into a table leg. When he begins to do so, a little voice cries, "No, you hurt me!" (I'm not making this up.) Every time he tries to carve the wood, it cries out in pain. Eventually, Mastro gives up and offers the log to his friend Geppetto, who makes wooden dolls. Geppetto carves out young Pinocchio and teaches him to walk and talk, and soon he runs off to town. There, the cops—who end up throwing poor old Geppetto into jail because it is said he doesn't like children and therefore must have been abusing Pinocchio—pick him up.

While Geppetto is in jail on false accusations, Pinocchio returns home alone and hungry. There he meets a talking cricket, which just happens to have been living in the house for nearly fifty years. The cricket explains to him that he has been misbehaving and that little boys who don't obey their parents will grow up to be donkeys. Pinocchio gets upset with the talking cricket and throws a hammer at him and probably kills him, although he appears later in the story in the form of a ghost, a doctor, and then again as a cricket. Pinocchio then cries himself to sleep with his feet on the stove. When he wakes up, his feet have been burned off. But not to worry, because Geppetto has been released from jail and makes him some new feet. And that's only one small part of the story.

I don't know about you, but I don't see any of that in the lovable characters brought to life in the 1940 silver-screen version. In fact, after reading the original story, I imagined Pinocchio replacing Don Vito and Michael Corleone from the GODFATHER movies, sitting around scratching his chin and making profound statements like "Keep your friends close, but your enemies closer" or "Shall I remind you what I did to the cricket?"

While Pinocchio and his conscience Jiminy Cricket are very close in the Disney movie, the book paints a much different and perhaps more accurate picture. The conscience is a mysterious concept that's difficult to understand and even more difficult to ignore. At times, most of us want to throw a hammer at our conscience and lay it to rest forever. After all, life would be easier without it. Or would it? Be careful, because if you dismiss conscience enough, It can become a faint voice off in the distance that never catches your attention.

I believe that following God closely can sensitize your heart and mind to any red flags your conscience might wave. In Scripture, the conscience always serves to caution the individual, never excuse behavior.

Focus

In the end, the point of the "how to believe" grid is much bigger than the elephants in the room. The more you understand your freedom, the more insignificant and small the elephants become. They no longer dominate the room or the discussion, but afford us the ability to focus on what matters — righteousness and peace and joy in the Holy Spirit. Freedom clears the air and keeps us from chasing our tails in the dark. As Christians, we should be the most free and focused people on the planet, living our lives to the audience of one.

Focus should also prevent us from bickering and fighting among ourselves, because it reminds us that we're on the same side. During the War of 1812, Andrew Jackson was a major in the Tennessee militia. At one point, the morale of the troops had reached an all-time low. They were constantly arguing, talking bad about each other, and fighting among themselves. Jackson pulled the troops together when tensions were at their worst and said, "Gentlemen! Let's remember, the enemy is over *there!*"[4]

While we live in a culture with an abundance of denominations and movements, grace demands that we focus on the King of the universe and never make an enemy out of each other. When we make enemies of each other, the real Enemy wins.

Advancing the Kingdom

A proper understanding of freedom will contribute to seeing others as infinitely valuable. Grace demands of us that we don't keep the message of Jesus to ourselves. The apostle Paul made it clear that a life *in Christ* will be busy with the ministry of reconciliation.

A few years ago I had an experience more convicting than any sermon I had ever heard preached. During my college years I had an inaccurate view of what being a minister of the gospel is all about. I thought too highly of the lights and screens and a poster that had my face on it; truth be known, I thought too highly of myself. Recognizing this in me, my father took me to Uganda, Africa, upon graduation, where we were to spend a couple of weeks serving local churches and villages. We were part of a team that was half preachers and half nurses and doctors. Each day, we'd walk through villages sharing the gospel and inviting people to the church to get connected to the community and receive medical help.

One morning after about an hour of walking, we came upon a hut with a mother and child sitting in front. I asked, through my interpreter, if we could have a conversation. She politely agreed. At that point I sat on the ground in front of her, something men would never do in her culture, and began to explain the message of Jesus. I drew in the dirt as I talked so she could have a visual to go along with what I was saying. After some questions and great discussion, she crossed the line of faith and became a Christ follower. We took her information for the church we were serving and continued to the next hut.

No less than twenty-five minutes later, we happened upon a hut with three mothers sitting in front and several children playing close by. We engaged them in conversation and began sharing Jesus. Not long into the presentation, my interpreter stopped me and said, "I am sorry, my brother, but we have already been here." He pointed me to a presentation written in the dirt about five feet away. Recognizing our confusion, the women began to giggle and point to the hut behind them. There, hiding in the shadows was the young mother who had become a Christian only twenty-five minutes earlier. She had been running through her village drawing the gospel message in front of each hut.

I was moved beyond what any words could describe and sat for a few moments marveling at a young mother who had been set free. In some circles, the idea of sharing your faith has become controversial and even taboo. And while God hasn't called us to be spiritual headhunters, he has called us to the ministry of reconciliation. It's not optional; grace demands it.

Glorifying God

Glorifying God is a commitment to what God cares about. Yes, God cares about people, social injustice, the big and small things . . . and the list goes on. But he highly esteems his own glory. John Piper worded it well: "Many people are willing to be God-centered as long as they feel that God is man-centered."[5] However, God expects us to glorify him no matter how small or big the issue may be. Paul said, "So eat your meals heartily, not worrying about what others say about you — you're eating to God's glory, after all, not to please them. As a matter of fact, do everything that way, heartily and freely to God's glory" (1 Corinthians 10:31-32, MSG).

Don't miss this. As we discuss and think through the decision-making grid in relation to gray areas and secondary issues, nothing is more important than bringing glory to God. That's crucial.

Intimacy with Christ

This might be the most fitting place to end our freedom journey—at the feet of Jesus. When properly understood, grace and freedom leave the single option of a God-centered life.

I hope freedom has helped you find clarity for the gray secondary issues of life. A few months ago my wife gave birth to our third child, Mercy Sophia Crowe. I stayed with my wife while she was in the hospital, so naturally when I came home, the other two children were ready for some "Daddy time." At our house, Daddy time usually involves burning off a lot of energy, laughing a lot, and getting pretty much whatever you want. I brought Charis and Gabe together and said, "If you could do whatever you want, what would it be?"

"To play in the pool!!!" they both shouted.

Did I mention it was March and the pool doesn't have a heater—and it was freezing? However, I didn't want to disappoint, so we got on our bathing suits and gathered at the edge of the water, looking at each other to see who would jump in first. My little girl spoke first: "One-Two-Three-Jump!" So there I went, an adult man jumping in freezing water to make a two- and three-year-old happy. When my head came out of the water, they both must have seen the look of shock on my face or I may have shouted something about the water temperature. Either way, after that neither of them would get in.

My son did invent a new game that involved him throwing a ball to me in the water, and me jumping to get it in a way that made the biggest splash. He laughed hysterically, which any dad will tell you is reward enough. It was a perfect moment, watching him standing at the edge of the pool, bending over, and then throwing his head back in joyous laughter.

Well, it was fun until the nightmare began. He threw his head back, and his little feet came out from under him. His head hit the side of the pool as he fell in. I rushed over, scooped him out of the water, and held him tightly against my chest as we moved to dry ground. Blood was everywhere, and even though I knew that is typical with a head wound, when it's your kid, "typical" doesn't matter. It didn't take long to realize we needed to make a trip to the emergency room. Upon arrival and check-in, I was told the wait would be three hours. Patience isn't a virtue I possess in the first place, and adding a gash in the back of my son's head into the mix, to say the least, made the situation tense. I don't know if it was the bribe I gave the woman taking our information or the fear she saw in my eyes, but within five minutes we were taken back.

The doctor came in, evaluated Gabe's wound, and informed me that a few staples would close the gash. He shared with me that prior to the staples, the back of Gabe's head needed to be numb, and a nurse would come in to give me further instructions. Moments later, a nurse came in and handed me a blue rubber glove and a cotton ball. She told me I'd need to apply numbing medicine to the cotton ball and hold my son down for twenty minutes as I shoved the cotton ball into the wound.

I looked at her and asked one simple question: "Are you on crack?" Trained to deal with hysterical dads, she smiled and let me know that this is the way it's done, and then she left the room.

I attempted to follow the instructions I'd been given, but I couldn't handle the tears and questions my son was asking about why I was holding him down. I removed the cotton ball from his wound, helped him down off the table he was lying on, and lay on the table myself. I then invited him to crawl up on my chest and lay his head down like he was going night-night. When I'm home, I try to rock my children before laying them down in their beds. So Gabe knew what I was talking about and climbed into my lap.

I put my arms around him and told him that I was going to have to touch his boo-boo. He immediately tensed up and cried. Then I began to slowly rock back and forth and sing him a song I had sung to him his entire life, the theme song from the ROCKY movies. As he listened to my voice with his head against my chest, there were no more tears, and he completely relaxed.

Grace leaves no other option but that we rest our head against the chest of our all-loving Father God. The reality is that there are zillions of issues we don't have a Bible reference for. Knowing how to believe in those gray areas allows us to say in the small things, "O God, you are my God, and I love you with all my heart, mind, soul, and strength."

Freedom is like the sun that burns away the early-morning fog, leaving a crystal clear perspective. When the fog of confusion and grayness is replaced with clarity, what awaits is what has always awaited us—a welcoming God.

When was the last time you rested your head against the Father's chest? Crawl up in his lap. Hear his heartbeat and rest. Experience the freedom that's yours.

NOTES

Introduction

1. It is significant to know that the death mentioned in this text is both an immediate spiritual death and an eventual physical death.

Chapter 1: Refrigerator Art

1. R. C. H. Lenski, *Commentary on the New Testament: 1–2 Corinthians* (Peabody, MA: Hendrickson, 2001), 1039.
2. S. Zodhiates, *The Complete Word Study Dictionary: New Testament,* electronic ed. (Chattanooga, TN: AMG, 2000), s.v. "kainos."
3. Lenski, 1039.
4. John Wesley, "John Wesley's Notes on the Bible," http://ewordtoday.com/comments/2corinthians/wesley/2corinthians5.htm (accessed March 25, 2006).
5. Zodhiates, s.v. "behold."
6. Wesley.
7. David E. Garland, *The New American Commentary: 2 Corinthians*, vol. 29 (Nashville: Broadman, Holman, 1999), 342.
8. Wayne Grudem, *Systematic Theology: An Introduction to Biblical Doctrine* (Grand Rapids, MI: Zondervan, 1995), 1253.
9. Zodhiates, s.v. "reconciliation."
10. Zodhiates, s.v. "reconciliation."
11. George Whitefield, *Selected Sermons of George Whitefield* (Oak Harbor, WA: Logos Research Systems, 1999).
12. James Swanson, *A Dictionary of Biblical Languages with Semantic Domains: Greek (New Testament)*, electronic ed. (Oak Harbor, WA: Logos Research Systems, 1997).
13. R. C. H. Lenski, *Commentary on the New Testament: 1–2 Corinthians* (Peabody, MA: Hendrickson, 2001), 1050.

Chapter 2: Meat, Idols, and Special Days

1. S. Zodhiates, *The Complete Word Study Dictionary: New Testament,* electronic ed. (Chattanooga, TN: AMG, 2000), s.v. "receive."

2. Craig Keener, *The IVP Bible Background Commentary: New Testament,* electronic ed. (Downers Grove, IL: InterVarsity, 1993).

3. John Calvin, *Calvin's Commentaries, Acts 14–28, Romans 1–16,* vol. XIX (Grand Rapids, MI: Baker, 2005), 494.

4. Calvin, 494.

5. William Barclay, *The Letter to the Romans,* electronic ed. (Louisville, KY: Westminster John Knox, 1975).

6. R. C. H. Lenski, *Commentary on the New Testament: Romans* (Peabody, MA: Hendrickson, 2001), 832.

7. Martin Luther, "Martin Luther's Bible Commentary," trans. Bro. Andrew Thornton, OSB, http://ewordtoday.com/comments/romans/luther/romans14.htm (accessed March 30, 2006).

8. Kenneth S. Wuest, *Wuest's Word Studies from the Greek New Testament: For the English Reader,* electronic ed. (Grand Rapids, MI: Eerdmans, 2002), s.v. "unhallowed."

9. Gerhard Friedrich, *Theological Dictionary of the New Testament* (Grand Rapids, MI: Eerdmans, 1985).

10. Lenski, 837.

11. R. Mounce, *The New American Commentary: Romans,* vol. 27 (Nashville: Broadman, Holman, 2001).

12. Warren Wiersbe, *The Bible Exposition Commentary: New Testament,* vol. 1 (Colorado Springs, CO: Cook, 2001), 561.

13. Zodhiates, s.v. "διωκω."

14. Mounce.

15. Luther.

16. Graeme Goldsworthy, *Preaching the Whole Bible as Christian Scripture* (Grand Rapids, MI: Eerdmans, 2000), 228.

17. Other texts that can help us define who our neighbors are include 1 Corinthians 9:19-22; 10:24,33; 11:1; 13:5; Philippians 2:4-5; and Titus 2:9-10.

18. Mounce.

19. Keener.

Chapter 3: Liberty Meets Responsibility

1. Donald T. Phillips, *Lincoln on Leadership* (New York: Warner Books, 1992), 51–52.

2. John Wesley, *Letters of John Wesley*, ed. George Eayrs (London: Hodder and Stoughton, 1915), 423.

3. S. Zodhiates, *The Complete Word Study Dictionary: New Testament*, electronic ed. (Chattanooga, TN: AMG, 2000), s.v. "μάκελλον."

4. Timothy Friberg, Barbara Friberg, and Neva F. Miller, *Analytical Lexicon of the Greek New Testament*, electronic ed. (Dartmouth, MA: Baker, 2000).

5. Paige Patterson, *The Troubled Triumphant Church* (Eugene, OR: Wipf & Stock, 2002), 172.

6. Patterson, 174.

7. Jochem Douma, *The Ten Commandments: Manual for the Christian Life*, trans. Nelson D. Kloosterman (Phillipsburg, NJ: P&R, 1996), 105.

8. John Calvin, *Calvin's Commentaries: 1 Corinthians, 2 Corinthians*, vol. 20 (Grand Rapids, MI: Baker, 2005), 350.

Chapter 4: Christ Has Set Us Free

1. Carol Kelly-Gangi, ed., *Abraham Lincoln: His Essential Wisdom* (New York: Barnes & Noble, 2007), 25.

2. T. George, *The New American Commentary: Galatians*, vol. 30. (Nashville: Broadman, Holman, 2001).

3. R. Jamieson, *A Commentary, Critical and Explanatory, on the Old and New Testaments* (Oak Harbor, OH: Logos Research Systems, 1997).

4. S. Zodhiates, *The Complete Word Study Dictionary: New Testament*, electronic ed. (Chattanooga, TN: AMG, 2000), s.v. "katargenō."

5. Martin Luther, "Martin Luther's Bible Commentary," http://ewordtoday.com/comments/galatians/luther/galatians5.htm (accessed April 10, 2006).

6. R. Lenski, *Commentary on the New Testament: Galatians, Ephesians, Philippians* (Peabody, MA: Hendrickson, 2001), 273.

7. John Calvin, *Calvin's Commentaries: Galatians, Ephesians, Philippians, Colossians, 1 & 2 Thessalonians, 1 & 2 Timothy, Titus, Philemon*, vol. XXI (Grand Rapids, MI: Baker, 2005), 158.

8. Timothy Friberg, Barbara Friberg, and Neva F. Miller, *Analytical Lexicon of the Greek New Testament*, electronic ed. (Dartmouth, MA: Baker, 2000), s.v. "περιπατέω."

9. James Swanson, *Dictionary of Biblical Languages with Semantic Domains: Greek (New Testament)*, electronic ed. (Oak Harbor, OH: Logos Research Systems, 1997).

10. Swanson, 207–210.

11. Kenneth S. Wuest, *Wuest's Word Studies from the Greek New Testament: For the*

English Reader, electronic ed. (Grand Rapids, MI: Eerdmans, 2002), s.v. "prassō."

12. Wuest, s.v. "prassō."

13. Bob Reccord, *Beneath the Surface* (Nashville: Broadman, Holman, 2002), 26.

14. Joseph Lightfoot, ed., *St. Paul's Epistle to the Galatians: A Revised Text with Introduction, Notes, and Dissertations* (London: Macmillan, 1874).

Chapter 5: Asking the Right Questions

1. Francis A. Schaeffer, *How Should We Then Live?* (Old Tappan, NJ: Crossway, 1976), 23.

2. Bill Hybels, "Accepting Unusual Christians" (Romans 14), sermon, as heard by the author.

3. John S. Feinberg and Paul D. Feinberg, *Ethics for a Brave New World* (Wheaton, IL: Crossway, 1993), 43–44.

4. Feinberg and Feinberg.

5. Garry Friesen with J. Robin Maxon, *Decision Making and the Will of God* (Sisters, OR: Multnomah, 2004), 115.

6. Friesen, 124.

7. Friesen, 134.

8. Graeme Goldsworthy, *Preaching the Whole Bible as Christian Scripture* (Grand Rapids, MI: Eerdmans, 2000), 240.

9. Wayne Grudem, *Systematic Theology: An Introduction to Biblical Doctrine* (Grand Rapids, MI: Zondervan, 1994), 643.

10. Daniel Akin, "God's Guidelines for the Gray Areas of Life," August 3, 2004, http://apps.sebts.edu/president/?p=136 (accessed February 9, 2010).

11. Paige Patterson, *The Troubled Triumphant Church* (Eugene, OR: Wipf & Stock, 2002), 104.

12. This story is found in Exodus 7:8-13.

13. Martin Luther, *Concerning Christian Liberty,* THE HARVARD CLASSICS, vol. XXXVI, part 6 (New York: P. F. Collier & Son, 1909–1914), 14, http://www.bartleby.com/36/6/2.html.

14. Luther, 1.

15. Feinberg and Feinberg.

16. C. S. Lewis, *Letters to an American Lady* (Grand Rapids, MI: Eerdmans, 1971), 40.

17. William Fraser McDowell, et al, *The Picket Line of Missions* (New York: Eaton and Mains, 1897), 40.

18. John Piper, *Desiring God* (Sisters, OR: Multnomah, 2003), 56.

Chapter 6: Elephant 1: Homosexuality

1. Michael Luo and Christina Capecchi, "Lutheran Group Eases Limits on Gay Clergy," *The New York Times,* August 21, 2009, http://www.nytimes.com/2009/08/22/us/22lutherans.html.

2. Andrew Sullivan, *Virtually Normal* (New York: Vintage, 1996), ix.

3. William Lane Craig, *Hard Questions, Real Answers* (Wheaton, IL: Crossway, 2003), 133–134.

4. John S. Feinberg and Paul D. Feinberg, *Ethics for a Brave New World* (Wheaton, IL: Crossway, 1993.)

5. John Calvin, *Calvin's Commentaries: Genesis*, vol. 1 (Grand Rapids, MI: Baker, 2005), 497.

6. R. L. Harris, G. L. Archer, and B. K. Waltke, *Theological Wordbook of the Old Testament,* electronic ed. (Chicago: Moody, 2003) .

7. Craig, 135.

8. W. A. Elwell and P. W. Comfort, *Tyndale Bible Dictionary*, electronic ed. (Wheaton, IL: Tyndale, 2001).

9. W. Wiersbe, *Be Holy* (Wheaton, IL: Victor, 1994).

10. G. J. Wenham, J. A. Motyer, D.A. Carson, and R. T. France, eds., *New Bible Commentary: 21st Century Edition*, rev. ed., electronic ed. (Downers Grove, IL: InterVarsity, 1994).

11. Wenham, Motyer, Carson, and France.

12. Jochem Douma, *The Ten Commandments: Manual for the Christian Life*, trans. Nelson D. Kloosterman (Phillipsburg, NJ: P&R, 1996), 270.

13. David Kinnaman and Gabe Lyons, *unChristian* (Grand Rapids, MI: Baker, 2007), 102.

14. Kinnaman and Lyons, 92.

15. Kinnaman and Lyons, 91–92.

Chapter 7: Elephant 2: The Cyber World

1. Internet World Stats: Usage and Population Statistics, http://www.internetworldstats.com/stats.htm (accessed February 10, 2010).

2. Augustine, *Confessions,* book 8 (New York: Oxford University Press, 2009).

3. C. S. Lewis, *The Weight of Glory* (New York: HarperCollins, 2001), 26.

4. C. S. Lewis, "Cross Examination," *God in the Dock* , ed., Walter Hooper (Grand Rapids, MI: Eerdmans, 1963), 262.

Chapter 8: Elephant 3: Social Drinking

1. I. H. Marshall, A. R. Millard, J. I. Packer, and Donald J. Wiseman, eds., *New Bible Dictionary*, 3rd ed., electronic ed. (Downers Grove, IL: InterVarsity, 1996), 1242.

2. Marshall, Millard, Packer, and Wiseman, 1243.

3. Daniel B. Wallace, "The Bible and Alcohol," http://bible.org/article/bible-and-alcohol (accessed August 28, 2009).

4. Wallace.

5. R. Jamieson, A.R. Fausset, A.R. Fausset, D. Brown, & D. Brown, *A Commentary, Critical and Explanatory, on the Old and New Testaments* (Oak Harbor, WA: Logos Research Systems, 1997), Proverbs 23:31.

6. C. F. Keil and F. Delitzsch, *Commentary on the Old Testament: Proverbs, Ecclesiastes, Song of Songs*, vol. 6 (Peabody, MA: Hendrickson, 2001), 347.

7. D. A. Garrett, *The New American Commentary: Proverbs, Ecclesiastes, Song of Songs*, vol. 14 (Nashville: Broadman, Holman, 2001), Proverbs 23:35.

8. Robert H. Stein, "Wine-Drinking in New Testament Times," http://www.swartzentrover.com/cotor/bible/Doctrines/Holiness/Drugs%20&%20Alcohol/Wine-Drinking%20in%20New%20Testament%20Times.htm (accessed March 8, 2010).

9. John Piper, "Flesh Tank and Peashooter Regulations," Colossians 2:16-23, January 17, 1982, http://www.desiringgod.org/ResourceLibrary/Sermons/ByDate/1982/330_Flesh_Tank_and_Peashooter_Regulations/ (accessed February 10, 2010).

10. John Piper, "I Will Not Be Enslaved by Anything," September 1, 1985, http://www.desiringgod.org/ResourceLibrary/Sermons/ByDate/1985/505_I_Will_Not_Be_Enslaved_by_Anything/ (accessed February 10, 2010).

Chapter 9: Elephant 4: Entertainment

1. Brian Godawa, *Hollywood Worldviews: Watching Films with Wisdom and Discernment* (Downers Grove, IL: InterVarsity, 2002), 10.

2. William E. Brown, *Where Have All the Dreamers Gone?* (Cedarville, OH: Cedarville University Press, 2003), 12.

3. C. S. Lewis, *God in the Dock,* "Myth Became Fact" (Grand Rapids, MI: Eerdmans, 1994), 66–67.

4. Godawa, 32, 43.

5. Neil Postman, *Amusing Ourselves to Death* (New York: Penguin Books, 1985), 10.

6. An idea expressed by Bill Brown in a lecture given on worldview and entertainment as heard by the author, summer 2009.

7. C. S. Lewis, *Selected Literary Essays,* "Hamlet: The Prince or the Poem," ed. Wester Hooper (Cambridge, England: Cambridge University Press, 1942), 104–105.

8. www.screenit.com is a subscriber site, but if you scroll to the bottom of the page, you can click "no thanks" to view reviews for free. You just have to wait one week for new-release reviews.

9. Robert K. Johnston, *Reel Spirituality: Theology and Film in Dialogue* (Grand Rapids, MI: Baker, 2006), 33.

10. Beverly Beyette, "A Modern-Day Schindler Faces the Consequences," *Los Angeles Times,* August 19, 1998, http://articles.latimes.com/1998/aug/19/news/ls-14350?; and Johnston, 34–35.

11. Brian Godawa articulated these basic elements of storytelling in chapter 2 of *Hollywood Worldviews.*

12. R. K. Harrison, ed. *Encyclopedia of Biblical and Christian Ethics* (Nashville: Thomas Nelson, 1987), 85.

13. Harrison, 85.

14. Dietrich Bonhoeffer, *Ethics* (New York: Simon & Schuster, 1955), 68.

Chapter 10: Elephant 5: Humanitarian Efforts

1. David Aikman, *Great Souls* (Nashville: Word, 1998), 195.

2. Aikman, 192.

3. William Barclay, *The Daily Study Bible Series: The Gospel of Matthew,* vol. 1 (Louisville, KY: Westminster John Knox, 1975), 182.

4. Content gathered from reading Bono's speech manuscript ("Transcript: Bono remarks at the National Prayer Breakfast," February 2, 2006, http://www.usatoday.com/news/washington/2006-02-02-bono-transcript_x.htm) and watching the speech at http://www.youtube.com/watch?v=gUdrYDk8rVA (accessed August 30, 2009).

5. Mark Galli and Ted Olson, *131 Christians Everyone Should Know* (Nashville: Broadman, Holman, 2000), 83.

Conclusion

1. Robert Fulghum, *All I Really Need to Know I Learned in Kindergarten* (New York: Ballantine Books, 1988), 81–83.

2. John C. Maxwell, *The Winning Attitude* (Nashville: Thomas Nelson, 1992), 24.

3. James M. Washington, ed. *A Testament of Hope: The Essential Writings and Speeches of Martin Luther King Jr.* (New York: HarperCollins, 1986), 120.

4. Charles R. Swindoll, *The Tale of the Tardy Oxcart* (Nashville: Word, 1998), 213.

5. John Piper, *Brothers, We Are Not Professionals* (Nashville: Broadman, Holman, 2002), 6.

ABOUT THE AUTHOR

BRENT CROWE is a thought-provoking visionary and speaker who engages such issues as leadership, culture, and change. He speaks to tens of thousands across the nation and abroad each year and is currently serving as the vice president of Student Leadership University, a program that has trained more than 50,000 students to commit themselves to excellence.

Brent is married to Christina and has three children: Gabriel, Charis, and Mercy. He holds two master's degrees from Southeastern Baptist Theological Seminary: a Master of Divinity in Evangelism and a Master of Arts in Ethics.

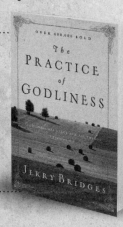
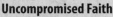

SUPPORT THE MINISTRY OF THE NAVIGATORS

The Navigators' calling is to advance the Gospel of Jesus and His Kingdom into the nations through spiritual generations of laborers living and discipling among the lost.

Navigators have invested their lives in people for more than 75 years, coming alongside them life-on-life to help them passionately know Christ and to make Him known.

The U.S. Navigators' ministry touches lives in varied settings, including college campuses, military bases, downtown offices, and urban neighborhoods, prisons, and youth camps.

Dedicated to helping people navigate spiritually, The Navigators aim to make a permanent difference in the lives of people around the world. The Navigators help their communities of friends to follow Christ passionately and equip them effectively to go out and do the same.

To learn more about donating to The Navigators' ministry,
go to **www.navigators.org/us/support**
or call toll-free at **1-866-568-7827**.